TOUCH: MAKING CONTACT
WITH CLIMATE CHANGE

by

Ben Cromwell

To Raven with love

and

To Ezra with hope

TABLE OF CONTENTS

ACKNOWLEDGEMENTS

I would like to thank Steve Tatum, Terry Tempest Williams and Francois Camoin for their input and guidance on this project. I would also like to thank Julia Corbett for her criticism and support. Many thanks to those friends and family members who bravely read through various drafts of this document and offered suggestions. Finally, I am indebted to Lindsy Floyd for her insight and inspiration. Without her, this project would not be half of what it is. Thanks are also due to *Canary in the Cole Mine* for publishing an early draft of "To My Love: An Incantation," to *Sage* for its publication of "Turtles," and to *Flyway* for graciously agreeing to publish "I Don't Give a Damn About Climate Change!" under the title "Touch." Many thanks indeed.

PREFACE

I have struggled writing this book. I'm telling you this upfront because the chapters that follow are not the book I intended to write. I suspect it may not be the book you intend to read either.

The book I wanted to write was published in 2009. It was written by David Orr and it is called *Down to the Wire*. It is a beautifully written and concise book, far better and larger in scope than I could have written. It discusses the political and cultural issues surrounding climate change, and it also covers some of the basic science behind the phenomenon.

For those wishing to read a precise account of the scope of this global disaster we so innocently call climate change, Orr's book is the place to start.

My own book contains none of Orr's insights into the phenomenon itself, or almost none. I have gone into very little detail about the causes of climate change, or, as Orr calls it, "the long emergency," and I have done my best to avoid simply regurgitating Orr's brilliantly articulated discussion of culture and politics.

I read *Down to the Wire* while going to school for a degree in Environmental Humanities at the University of Utah. I had been thinking, for some time, about the nature of global warming, and decided that the real problem lay not in carbon emissions or fossil fuel consumption, but in the way human beings approach the world. Our governments, economies, wars, our ideas about family and community, and even our simplest unconscious decisions like what to eat or wear, in short, our cultures, not just American culture, but all human cultures, seemed, to me, to feed into a mentality that inevitably lead towards environmental destruction. That was what I was hoping to talk about: why we're so screwed up. *Down to the wire* is not quite as cynical as all that, but as I read it in January of 2010, it seemed to reinforce all my intuitive understanding of climate change. It was both an extremely satisfying and extremely frustrating experience. Here was everything I wanted to say in a form both more coherent and more readable than I'd ever been able to achieve.

Reading Orr's book was, however, a turning point for me. I realized that there were other, more qualified people writing about the science, politics, and economics of climate change. My book would have to be about something altogether different, something that only I could tell.

Touch is that book. It is about how climate change has affected me, physically, mentally, spiritually, and emotionally. It is an attempt to reckon the impact that climate change can have in the course of a single life.

In coming to terms with those impacts, many other people who are close to me and many issues normally considered to be beyond the scope of climate activists have come into play. Because of that, this book is both personal and flawed.

Much of what I have written is from memory, and I must apologize to those people who will read this book and remember the events I've recounted here in a different light. I ask them to consider the possibility that I am not altogether wrong.

I must apologize, too, to those readers, some who are members of my own family, who do not believe that climate change exists or that it is primarily caused by the activities of human beings. You are wrong. 97% of scientists who study the issue and publish peer reviewed articles on it agree that the climate is changing and that the changes are mostly due to human activities. Of the three percent who remain, some are simply honest scientists who remain unconvinced by the evidence, but most are on the payrolls of companies who have vested interests in fossil fuels. They do not want you to believe in Climate Change because it will hurt their bottom lines. Their motivations are simple: they care more about money and power than about your life (or their own lives for that matter).

I have written this entire book under the assumption that my audience accepts the facts, and believes that the world is warming and that our climate is becoming fundamentally unstable as a result. If that does not describe you, you may not enjoy this book. I encourage you to read it anyway. Additionally, I suggest *What We Know about Climate Change* by Kerry Emanuel. If you are still skeptical after reading all of this, go outside and see for yourself. Talk to your friends and neighbors about their observations of the natural world, the trees in their yards, the plants in their gardens, the birds visiting their feeders. Evidence of climate change is all around you if you pay attention.

Despite my apologies, I believe that this book is important. It is most certainly important to me, and I can't help but think that it is important for my audience as well. As far as I know, no one has yet attempted to write a personal account of how climate change is beginning to show up in his or her daily life, yet that is precisely what we need in order to begin to take this problem seriously.

I have written this book in the hope that my story will be like a mirror. I believe this project asks that you examine your own life, and how it has been affected by this pervasive disaster.

Finally, this book is a shot in the dark. I do not honestly believe that we, as human beings, will be able to reverse the effects of climate change in time to avoid unspeakable disaster. I believe many people will die as a result of climate change, and that the survivors will lead diminished lives. I am almost sure our species will not be able to recover from the massive amounts of damage we've done to the Earth.

But I could be wrong. I hope I am wrong. Please, let me be wrong.

Ben Cromwell
Salt Lake City, 2011

HOW WE GOT HERE

In the beginning was the word and the word was
with God, and the word was God.
　　　–John 1:1 (NIV)

How did you get here? Close your eyes and
surrender.
　　　– Rumi

I was sitting near the window of the plane as it
banked for the first time in hours. It was around
midday, the sun was right overhead, and as I looked
out, I caught sight of Kiribati for the first time.
There are no mountains in the country, no wide
open spaces. The first impression I had was that
someone had spilled some green, leafy oil in the
ocean and that it was swirling just above the surface
of the water in long, thin streaks. It was a ribbon so
thin I wondered whether I wasn't simply seeing a
barrier island far off the coast, that we would bypass
this sandbar and go on towards the real island, but
then I caught sight of the runway, a flat,
blacktopped slash through the trees, and we were
circling lower and lower…
　　　– excerpted from my journal
　　　(8th March, 2006)

I am writing mythology. Origin myths.

How we came to be here. The Bible says with great

confidence, "In the beginning God created the

heavens and the Earth." I like the simplicity, the forthright tone of the statement. Perhaps I should begin in a like manner. I've been doing some creating of my own, you see. My wife is pregnant. Soon, I will have a son. That's where this begins, with creation in the midst of vast, unimaginable, global destruction.

How did we get here? The short answer is I don't know. No one is very sure about that, in fact. It has something to do with greenhouse gasses, and more to do with political history, and some to do with greed, imperialism, evolution, genetics, instinct... All the things that make us human, in short, brought us to this point.

Another question: How did I get here, to the point of telling creation stories? That, I can answer more precisely. I am having a son. Somewhere in my mind, this fact, this one beautiful insistence in the whole matrix of seven billion heaving bodies, seven billion pumping hearts, seven billion minds firing off billions more electrons, this one life that has barely begun makes a difference. I will be a father. Something has shifted.

I believe my son needs to know something of my thoughts, something of what is important to me, what makes me who I am, and what will ultimately shape him. Because my beliefs will shape his for better or worse; I must have them out, here and now.

In 2006, I joined the Peace Corps with my wife, Raven, and we were stationed in Kiribati[1]. We spent close to two years on the island of Abaiang which is in the Gilbert Islands. If you're looking at a world map, find the equator and follow it to the middle of the Pacific, just west of the international dateline. Find Tarawa, the capital of Kiribati and head north to the next island. That tiny green speck, which may or may not be labeled depending on the quality of your map, is Abaiang. It is going underwater.

---

[1] Pronounced Kiribas. The "ti" in Kiribati words makes an "s" sound. One legend tells that the first missionary to Kiribati brought with him a typewriter to transcribe the language, but that the "s" was broken and he was forced to improvise.

There are conflicting reports about this. The University of New Zealand has recently undertaken a study in which satellite imagery is being compared with aerial photos of Pacific atolls from World War Two. Initial findings indicate that many of them seem to be growing despite an overall sea level rise of nearly an inch (Lilly). No one is quite sure how this is happening and speculation abounds. Some people theorize that the increase in size is due to increases in built infrastructure. In Male, the capital of the Maldives, for instance, people have been building causeways and seawalls for years in an attempt to reclaim land from the sea, but on some islands the cause of growth is unclear.

People disagree about how quickly and how much sea levels will rise within the next fifty years. Some say the rise will be six inches, some say three feet.

What people do agree on is that either of those values is enough to outpace the growth of coral atolls, and that most of the country of Kiribati will be underwater fifty years from now, and the hundred thousand or so inhabitants will have to move.

I had heard about climate change before I joined the Peace Corps, but I can't remember where. It may have been in high school or earlier than that. I knew that it was a huge disaster and that I'd better recycle, better turn off lights when I left a room, better burn less gas, but it wasn't a threat, really. It wasn't immediate. It was like the destruction of the Amazon Rainforest. You shake your head and say "terrible, terrible" and then you move on. The problem was remote and easy to ignore.

Don't get me wrong, I was never a skeptic. I believed what scientists were saying about global warming. The Earth's average temperature is increasing. The ice caps are melting. Polar bears are going extinct. Tropical diseases are becoming more prevalent. The seas are rising. And I was alarmed by the whole thing to be sure, but the world is filled with sad news. People get murdered. Natural disasters occur. Genocide happens.

There's a lot of noise out there and it's difficult to focus on one disaster when there are ten screaming at you from the front page of the newspaper every day.

In Kiribati, climate change came home for me. There is no better way to put this. I fell in love with that place. I fell in love with the people, the beautiful brown of their skin, the silky black of their hair, the unique rhythm and timbre of the language. I fell in love with the culture, the way life seemed to move more slowly, the way important issues were taken to a council of elders and publicly discussed, the way they were never quite settled as though there was room for doubt in every decision. Nothing was absolute. It was democracy as I'd never seen it practiced. I fell in love with my village, the stick homes and buia's, the cinder block classrooms, the way all of it seemed nestled into the surrounding landscape, the way the villagers had to beat back the encroaching vegetation, the way each compound had its own banana and papaya and coconut tree, the way fresh fruit and toddy was a part of the diet without anyone even being conscious of eating healthy. I fell in love with my dog, my cats, my house, my neighbors, the students I taught. All of it was so real, so green and vibrant. I lived there and it existed and I loved it. And it is threatened.

This place of mine, that I have inside of me, this place made of coconut twine and pandanus logs and thatch, of sapphire ocean and emerald lagoon, and blood red sunset, and water as far as the eye can see, this fragile place where everything seemed so isolated, so fresh and novel, this place that I learned by heart will disappear within fifty years, and the friends I made there will be among the first people on Earth to lose their entire country. This is more than a global disaster. This is personal.

Part of me knows that I can't stop the oceans from rising, but the other part of me, which is considerably smaller and less rational, wants to try.

Another revelation came to me recently, not a revelation of an idea, but one of flesh and bone: my son. I can't see him yet, or hold him, but he's there just below the surface, a human life magiced into existence inside of my wife. Already, he has our DNA, and when I imagine him, it is Raven's green eyes I see, her dark hair, her long, elegant neck. I imagine he has her personality, too, her strong will, her insistence on fairness and honesty, her biting sense of humor, her compassion, all the twists and turns of her body. I know no other way to love. They are bound together, mother and son, two people contained in one, and her body, right now, protects his, but they are not the same person, however intertwined they seem. I dread his birth, when the two will separate, and his tiny, naked, fragile body will finally be exposed. If only I could take him inside of me. If only he could stay there forever.

Kiribati is an entire country. It is difficult to destroy an entire country. My son is infinitely more vulnerable. I am worried that this disaster, the mass destabilization of the Earth's climate, will wreak more kinds of destruction on us than we have anticipated. If Kiribati goes under, a hundred thousand people far away get moved across the ocean to a country they're unprepared to live in. No one or, at least very few people, will die. But if the seas do rise enough to flood Kiribati, won't they also flood the United States? I've heard reports that up to a third of Louisiana could go underwater. Much of Florida and Mississippi, not to mention the Atlantic states, will become unlivable. Our entire country will be irrevocably changed, and where will the people who live there go?

And if that disaster can happen, what about the predictions that plagues of tropical disease could move North, beyond the borders of Mexico and the Caribbean? What about the predicted food shortages due to drought and changing weather patterns? Will the United States remain a functioning democracy if part of the population cannot find enough food? There is a distinct possibility that very few of us will survive.

My son is vulnerable. And yet, he is strong, too. He is a blank slate, unbiased and unsullied. There is no life to which he has become accustomed. He has nothing to lose while I have everything to lose. His power and mine lie there, within those facts.

I believe there is a way to live that will do no more harm. I believe there is a way to live that will begin to repair the damage, to reverse these terrible things. My intent, in writing this book, is to find that way. My intent is to share it with my son and with you. My intent is survival, our survival.

The problem is that, for most of us, climate change remains remote. Even for me, though I have seen the immediacy of it, the destruction, climate change exists somewhere in the distance. It is surreal and ethereal, a fading memory. The stories that follow are a way to make contact with climate change, with the fabric of it, both physically and emotionally. They are a way to place my fingers in the wound and remember.

We are dying. May this be resurrection.

*   *   *

Begin again.

Touch

When I was growing up, my dad used to tell stories. My mom told stories, too, and read to me almost every night, but it was my father's tales that intrigued me. Almost all of them were horror stories. My favorite was about the Lake Carlisle monster. The story was about a father and his son who go camping out at Lake Carlisle in Illinois. They're driving in their pickup truck when all of a sudden, a pair of glowing yellow eyes appears in front of them in the darkness. They stop and approach the monster whose only words are, "I know who you are." The man and his son try to shine flashlights on the beast, but he remains shadowy and indistinct. They try to talk to it, but the monster only repeats his pronouncement in a sinister low growl. "I know who you are." Eventually the monster disappears and the man and boy drive off, shaken but unharmed.

Other stories my father told me were about equally disturbing phenomenon, an alien on a space shuttle, a ghost cougar, and a tiger that no one except my father ever saw. There was only a paw print the size of a dinner plate and some missing goats for proof. The last two of these stories were set in Nepal, and I found out only later that the story about the tiger was true... or partially true.

During his Peace Corps service, my dad did find a tiger track on the road to his house. It was enormous and clearly feline, but none of the villagers believed him. He was stationed in the northern part of Nepal in a remote area in the foothills of the Himalayas where tigers are almost unheard of. He never saw the cat, but there was the mysterious paw print, a strange remnant from an invisible threat.

When I was older, I became fascinated with my dad's Peace Corps stories, true tales of sometimes near death experiences that had occurred in the distant past before I was born. I heard about the time he came down with typhoid fever and nearly died before a friend of his was able to trek to a village with a radio and call in a helicopter. I heard about a stream crossing near dark when he waded out into the water and then realized the

Touch

current was too strong for him to take another step forward or back, and how he was rescued by a Nepali man who happened along the path in the nick of time. I heard about his science and math classes in open air classrooms crowded with Nepali students sitting cross legged on the floor.

All of this was fascinating to me and I dreamed that one day I, too, would be able to join the Peace Corps and travel to strange countries where it was still possible to participate in Indiana Jones like adventures. So, in February of 2006, I went to Kiribati as an education volunteer with the Peace Corps. I had gotten married six months previously, and my dad had pulled me aside a month or so before we left to give me a piece of advice.

"Your Peace Corps experience is going to be very different from mine," he said. "You have a wife and your first priority is to take care of her. You can't forget that." I nodded.

"I won't."

Raven and I realized we were unprepared for our posting twenty-four hours before we reached Kiribati. We had a layover in Fiji. We arrived there after a fifteen hour flight across the Pacific. It was near midnight when we landed. Everyone was excited. We were on a tropical island and we were at the start of something exciting, Peace Corps service.

And then the door of the plane opened and the cabin was immediately filled with the most uncomfortable hot sticky air. It made our skin crawl after the air conditioned plane ride. We gathered our things and made our way down the steps to the tarmac. It was the dead of night, the air was still and it was unbearably hot. We went to the hotel the Peace Corps had arranged for us, and every volunteer immediately went inside and turned on the air conditioning. Raven and I undressed and laid down on the bed and let the cool dry air stream over us until we were comfortable again.

"Shit," I said. "Maybe this was a mistake." We lay there looking up at the ceiling as the romance of our adventure dissolved outside in the sweltering humidity

TO MY LOVE: AN INCANTATION

I.

I am disappearing. It's only been three days since I left Salt Lake, but she is forgetting me, my face. She said so last night and I told her to find a picture of me, but I knew it wouldn't help. I am not there and love is so much physical, not just skin on skin, but the weight of her beside me, the movement of breath that I can feel from one end of the apartment to the other. I'm in Centennial Valley, Montana. Two weeks. No big deal, but it's more time apart than we'd like, more time than we've been apart in three years, and the weight of separation sits heavy on us. Raven and I have recently finished hiking the Appalachian Trail together. Two hundred miles, the last leg from Mount Katahdin to Little Bigelow Peak, and we were never more than a hundred feet apart. Now, we're in different states, and I feel as though I'm disappearing, as though I only exist when we are together.

I stand in the grass outside my cabin in the thick morning fog. The sun has not yet risen, though there is a soft golden glow indicating the horizon. I am in a bird sanctuary so there must be birds, hundreds of them, but they don't stir and neither do I. Instead, I let the cold mist wash over me. I close my eyes and I might as well be a deer standing stock still or a willow that stirs only with the breeze. I become indistinct, a part of a still, dark landscape. The sun slips silently over the horizon, and I open my eyes to brilliantly orange fog. A door creaks on rusty hinges nearby. I shake the cold from my limbs and step stiffly towards the cabin.

*   *   *

I did not hear about the oil spill for three days after it happened. I do not watch the news, so when my father told me about it, it was as if the whole thing was happening at warp speed. I forced myself to sit down at my computer and watch videos on CNN and MSNBC. There were aerial shots of the oil slicked gulf and, already, footage of gulls and cranes covered in tarry poison, but the image that sticks out for me is of a woman on a beach in front of a white building, her home and her business, a bed and breakfast on the coast. "I stand to lose everything," she says to the reporter interviewing her. I think to myself, Haven't we already?

In all the images I watched, I could not find the gulf. As a child, I'd been there on vacation with my family, to Fort Meyers, Ana Maria Island, Clearwater where we'd swum with manatees. I recall the soft, gritty feel of sand beneath my feet, walking down the beach for hours under the spell of breaking waves. I remember wading out beyond the breakers, the water lifting me gently off my feet, and at the crest, I could see pelicans and other ocean birds diving into the blue water, and, farther out, the fins of dolphins surfacing near the horizon like graceful loops of a sea serpent. I remember the wind blowing off the sea, the sky at sunset, reds and purples bleeding into the water. All of it is gone.

*   *   *

Touch

The oil spill will take lifetimes to recover from. There is so much death to be reckoned. Dead fish and dead birds and dead mammals. Dead species like the Smalltooth Sawfish which scientists are predicting may go extinct because of the spill. And there are other, still wider deaths. The news has made much of the fact that our trust in multinational oil companies is dying. Personally, I never had much trust in them to begin with. Trust in government, too, is very low, but there is another death I mean to get to, hard to talk about. Perhaps it is a death of the bigness of the universe, the idea that we could recover because there was still so much world and so much time. How many more of these can we absorb? I am disappearing with the gulf under a sheen of darkness.

*   *   *

I remember another ocean on the East coast. A beach at Chincoteague Island. It is raining, but not hard. A storm is moving out to sea and the waves are gray and turbid with the disturbance. I walk down the beach with my father. We are picking up crabs, giant horseshoe crabs that have been washed ashore by the storm. We cradle the crabs in our arms, each one the size of a dinner plate, and walk to the edge of the water pitching them as far out as we can. I feel the softness of their bodies underneath. We are saving them.

*   *   *

Begin again.

We met in the Ozarks of southern Missouri. She came into the office of the summer camp where I was working. The next day, I gave her a tour of the lake, the docks and cabins, the woods between. She was tall and beautiful, with long dark hair and huge gold-green eyes. I could barely look at her without sweating and trembling. She seemed nervous, too, though perhaps that was only because she was in a new place. After the tour, she went back to her room with two friends she'd brought along.

We began to exist for one another, to become substantial.

Touch

At first we were only eyebrows and fingernails, or silhouettes. Our minds can only brush the edges of reality with each contact, each experience filling in a bit more of the whole. You notice the silky hairs on the small of her back as she bends for a view of the lake, way the corners of her mouth are lined ever so slightly from smiling too often. Little by little you assemble her from the pieces. True creation takes time.

*   *   *

There is another beach that recurs endlessly in my mind, the shorelines of our village on Abaiang. Tanraake, Tanrio, ocean and lagoon, the blood red reef at dawn, the waves coming in like a host of starry eyed lovers.

The kids in Ueen Wakaam[2] used to tear the wooden tops off of their desks. I would see them at the beach, surfing the waves from the very edge of the reef into the shore, a distance that grew longer in September. A king tide hit and we lost three meters of beach. The trees nearest the shore turned

---

[2] Name of the village where we were stationed on Abaiang.

brown or fell as the beach eroded and salt water worked its way down into the water lens.[3] There was nothing to do but watch as the island slipped lower into a rising sea. We watched and tried to make the world exist as we had each other, by an act of pure will. Moment by moment, exist. And then we closed our eyes and prayed.

*   *   *

The island is sliding slowly seaward. The damage is done, no stopping it. Abaiang will crumble foot by foot into the water with each new high tide. Death by attrition.

Tebwake, our neighbor, disappeared, too, died of a sudden heart attack despite our arms around him, despite how much we wanted him to live. We could not save him, and we buried him beneath the sand at the edge of the island. Will they

---

[3] The water lens is a phenomenon that occurs on atolls. The porous coral the island is made of absorbs both rain water and salt water. Due to the difference in the density of fresh and salt water and the slow rate of mixing that occurs within the stone, a layer of fresh water sits on top of the salt water within the rock. Wells can be drilled into the water lens to access only the fresh water.

Touch

dig him up when the water rises, when it's time to leave for good?

*   *   *

This morning, I saw Chris Jordan's pictures of birds, albatross from midway. Dead birds, choked on pieces of plastic from the great Pacific trash heap. The birds fly out to sea and dive for food. They mistake the shiny plastic for fish scales and scoop up lighters, pens, bottle caps, toothbrushes, and return with them to their nests where they regurgitate the plastic to feed their young. The aftermath remains in the decomposing nests nestled in the low grasses of midway. Dead birds, both adults and chicks, their bones and feathers decomposing, becoming dirt again, their plastic insides, like negatives of prophecy. Bird entrails pointing towards a bleak future full of death, destruction, the birds themselves, gone.

In the full light of day, the Centennial Valley proves to be full of birds. The Red Rock lakes Wildlife Refuge is a story of restoration. In the 1800s accounts of the Centennial Valley relate stories of flocks of trumpeter swans so dense they blotted out the sun, but hunting and development near Yellowstone Park reduced their numbers to only 69 birds in 1932. The refuge was created to bring their numbers back up and in recent years, the population has climbed back to somewhere over 500 individuals.

This morning I can see no swans, but there are red-tailed hawks and bald eagles, short eared owls, black faced ibis, and a hundred others I can't identify. I look out at an abundance of avian life, and it is hard to believe in these photos of dead birds, hard to understand such destruction. We're so far from Midway. I don't want to believe my eyes.

But there is a truth to it. The things I've witnessed are related. Climate change, oil spills, plastic, heart failure. They are byproducts of prosperity, of apathy and greed, of a culture founded on consumption, of oil.

Touch

I sing of destruction and loss, effortless and simple. It's the law of the universe. Everything breaks down.

*   *   *

I am disappearing like Tebwake, like the birds, like Abaiang, dissolving into the background and leaving only poison, the hate filled guts of myself behind. These things are like erasers, like sandpaper. They take the smallest pieces of me with each contact.

She imagines me in the dark, and I imagine her in tiny bits like handfuls of sand. I put them back, carefully, one by one. "It's not your fault." "You are worthy." "I love you." Our voices are like psalms, our hands move over each other, slow, deliberate, mapping our own diminishment, repairing what we can, relearning the contours of our bodies, the reverse of vanishing.

II.

My wife gave me a stuffed yellow baby the first summer we dated. It was meant as a joke, and we both laughed when she told me it was our child. There was a longing in her voice, a hopefulness behind her eyes. I felt myself breaking open with love.

We are desert people, for our love grew there in the Sonoran. I was living in Scottsdale, which is a wreck of homes and golf courses, but it was still desert, still dry and hot and the yards carried a certain enchantment despite their concrete cages. Deserts can never really be contained by a city, still less mountains, and the medians of roads, vacant lots, and unwatered gardens were rife with toothy succulents like ocotillo, prickly pear and sand burrs. Scorpions made their way into the most secluded closets, and in the heart of Scottsdale, the serrated profile of Camelback Mountain loomed over the resorts and million dollar homes, a dragon lying in wait to devour tender, sunburned tourists.

Besides that, there were the 101 and 202 highways, bands of blacktop that separated the heart of the Phoenix metro area from the wasteland beyond. And yet, it was a connection for us. Just

45 minutes on the highway, and the waste began, and it was a waste of a magnificent kind. Fields of brown and orange rock dotted here and there with dry tufts of desert grass, palo verde, chollas, barrel cactus, and that most majestic of desert dwellers, the saguaro, to say nothing of the wildlife, diamondbacks as thick as a forearm, rose tarantulas, gila monsters, and all manner of small lizards and rodents. It was a paradise of a wasteland where only humans found it difficult to prosper.

That was where we spent our time, camping in washes near Lost Dutchman Mountain, wandering the open spaces of Scottsdale, inhabiting the dry air. It was here that we became a family. I don't know the physics of it, but there is something that occurs between people when they have loved enough and reveled enough and trusted deeply. Maybe it's not science, but a kind of alchemy of the spirit.

*   *   *

We had driven south on I-17 to Camp Verde and from there, east towards the Verde River. We rolled down the windows and tasted the dust as we bumped along down the steep, rocky road into the valley, relieved simply to be with one another, alone at last. The past two days had been spent in the presence of my extended family, my parents and sister, an aunt and uncle, and two cousins. It had been cold in the high desert near Flagstaff and my family can be trying, but as we lost altitude, the air began to warm to a pleasant temperature and the stress of such a high stakes meeting (it was Raven's first with my parents) began to melt away as the smell of water and cottonwoods intensified.

We set up our tent and hiked into the secluded hot springs up the valley. The water was warm and pleasant and we sat and held each other in the spring for several hours. On the way back, she stepped off the trail to pee and I walked farther on.

The cottonwoods hummed with the clicks of insects. Without knowing why, I turned too soon and saw her, her hair, the backs of her arms, the pale rounds of her bottom. She stood and let her

Touch

skirt fall and I could feel the brush of cloth upon my thighs. The wind in my hair.

That night, we lay together and could not distinguish between our own hands, whose skin was whose. We were composed of Earth and rocks and water and waxy cuticles. We were sharp and hard and soft and warm. The tent was our burrow and we were jackrabbits or desert mice contained in the flesh of the Earth.

III.

His eyes bulged, sticky and opaque, and the smell of him washed over us in the hot breeze. I keep returning here, to this death, the mouth filled with blow flies, the body swollen and pale with bacteria, death, and a kind of resurrection. And we put him back into the Earth. It was a healing. A way to make the whole thing right.

*   *   *

And the Pacific, what can we do with that? And the Gulf, where will we bury it?

*   *   *

Making Contact With Climate Change

My father and I walk slowly through the rain, and the crabs look like dinosaurs, or older than that. They are the very first things on Earth, the remnants of the Earth's first dreaming, when it dreamed strange and terrible things, shelled and spiked as if about to make war on itself, or on a vast celestial plane. They move their upturned legs like insects and their shells glow brown and gold in the gloaming. One by one, we right them, returning them to the sea because they are beautiful and helpless, because there is nothing else to do. And it's easy, the easiest thing in the world.

*   *   *

I've begun to write letters to my son, to call out to him and summon him as a witness, though he is still months away. Sometimes I tell him of his ancestors, what little I know, of where he came from. Sometimes, I write my sorrows, my worry that there will be no Earth for him, no home at all. These I burn because I must. I write to tell him of the beautiful things in the world fearing that there will be none left. And I write, too, out of hope.

Touch

That maybe we've saved something, maybe the crabs survived, and the skeletons of the birds were not the whole story. There were others that flew away.

And there are stories too, about live creatures huddled together in their dens, dreaming you.

TURTLES

The very simplicity and nakedness of man's life in
the primitive ages imply this advantage at least, that
they left him still but a sojourner in nature. […] But
lo! Men have become the tools of their tools.
— Thoreau

In Kiribati, I learned that the world is made
of turtles. This may be a metaphor. Actually, the
soil of tropical atolls is made up mostly of coral.
The islands sit atop ancient undersea ridges, formed
from volcanic activity and populated with tiny
microorganisms which secrete a hard exoskeleton
made of calcium carbonate. Because of this, the
soil on atolls is alkaline. Few plants grow well in
such soil. Coconut palms, saltbush, breadfruit trees,
and a strange tree called pandanus, with long
triangular serrated leaves, tend to thrive under such
conditions and so atolls in Kiribati are mostly
covered in dense jungles of these plants. All of the
plants I'm familiar with from my time there, except
saltbush, bear some sort of fruit. Coconuts are
familiar, but breadfruit and pandanus are both

strange. Breadfruit looks like a small green brain, kind of like an osage orange, but the tree is far larger, with a straight, brown barked trunk and huge symmetrical limbs radiating from it. Both the tree and the fruit emit a sticky white sap when lacerated. It is difficult to cut up a breadfruit because of this, but if you can manage it, fried breadfruit chips with a bit of salt taste better than French fries.

Pandanus, on the other hand, is not, primarily, a food plant. The plant, which looks like something Dr. Seuss would dream up, does produce a two feet in diameter sphere of hard green segments. One can break these segments off of a central hub and chew on the resulting pieces which resemble candy corns, the outer edge being green and the inner orange. The fruit tastes like a carrot and is fibrous and woody. Strands of it are apt to become lodged between teeth in a most uncomfortable manner. The trunk of the tree grows hundreds of dowel sized tendrils which extend straight out from the trunk and downward and act like buttresses to keep the tree upright. Several branches extend upward from the trunk as well and put out bunches of leaves like a palm tree. The leaves are serrated and razor sharp. The trunk of the tree is an important material for boat building and home construction and the leaves can be prepared into long flat sections and woven into mats and ceremonial clothing.

The relatively low diversity of plants on the island sits in marked contrast to the abundance of life in the sea. The reef is home to sea cucumbers, octopus, eels, clams, and all manner of fish while just beyond its edge dwell sharks, dolphins, deep sea species like tuna and snapper, and sea turtles. It is the turtles that intrigue me more than any other animal.

I never saw one in the wild, only after someone had caught one and set it, still alive, on its back outside the family compound. They were beautiful even on their backs, the diameter of dining room tables, huge and unwieldy. I used to ride past on the back of the transport truck and see them feebly moving their heads and flippers, the bodies too immense to do anything else.

Other times they were still. Where the head should have been, only a bloody stump. Their long, elegant flippers hanging limp.

Sea turtle meat is a delicacy in Kiribati, as it is in much of the world. People eat both the adults and the eggs in Indonesia, Mexico, China and many other places.

I couldn't bring myself to eat them, their flesh, the color of cooked chicken. They were supposed to be salty and tender, and some part of me wanted to taste them because it was new and exotic, because I knew I would never have another chance, but overwhelming instinct told me that it would be wrong.

Eating turtles is illegal. Most species of sea turtle are endangered, but they're easy to catch. They move slowly and gracefully through the water relying on their shells for protection. Fishermen just pull up alongside them and haul them over the lip of the boat. Turtles are also vulnerable to long line fishing and shrimp nets. The soft shelled eggs can simply be dug up and put into a bucket. They are easy pickings.

*   *   *

Turtle hunting isn't the only reason the population is endangered. Development, too, has caused a sharp decline in numbers. Most turtles return to the same beaches where they hatched to lay their eggs. Many of these nesting grounds have been and are being developed into seaside resorts. I recently spent Christmas in San Jose del Cabo. The resort I stayed at had a turtle hatchery. Workers had dug up nests of eggs and redeposited them behind a chain link fence to protect them from tourists recreating on the beach. When the turtles hatched, they put them all into an orange plastic bucket and brought them down near the ocean. Guests of the resort, myself included, were invited to help the baby sea turtles reach the ocean unharmed.

The marine reptiles were the size of a child's hand and fifteen of us watched about thirty turtles struggle over the sand toward the waves. After a

Touch

few minutes, the crowd got bored with this and people began to pick up the turtles in their hands and walk them out into the ocean.

I had misgivings about touching wild animals. I wanted to let them find their own way, but in no time there were only two turtles left and my wife, Raven, picked up the one nearest to me and put it in my hands.

"Thank you." I said, and I walked it out into the warm water and lowered it gently down until, with a twitch of tiny flippers it floated free of my hands and swam headlong for the breakers.

"I knew you wouldn't pick it up yourself," said Raven. I nodded.

I hadn't wanted to interfere. I worry, even now, that what we did may have killed more turtles than it saved. How will they know where to return having been harvested as eggs and transported in an orange bucket and then carried to the sea. Perhaps their struggle in the sand is necessary. Perhaps it gives them some sort of memory or skill they need to survive. Perhaps the smell of sunscreen on their leathery hides will attract predators. There are so many unknowns. Simpler just to know that they are there like doctrine, that they will always be there, and not to interfere.

The I-Kiribati had a special relationship with turtles. Christianity came to the islands in the 1800s alongside whaling vessels and fortune hunters. Before "first contact" with Europeans, the I-Kiribati were known for building the fastest boats in the Pacific. They ate mostly fish and breadfruit, no one wore clothes, and everyone was certain that the Earth, the oceans, the islands, and anything else that existed, did so on the backs of giant turtles[4].

Quite a lot of these practices have, now, been laid aside in favor of European influences. Wooden boats are being replaced with metal ones, rice is replacing breadfruit. It's rare, but not unheard of, for women to dance the traditional maie topless. Harder to shake, however, are the turtles.

---

[4] I have since learned that this tradition refers only to a specific island, ocean island which is located north of Kiribati, closer to Hawaii. Tabakea, the turtle was buried under that island in one creation myth and holds it on his back.

People in my village were either Catholic or Protestant. They attended church on Sundays and sang religious songs and tithed, but there was a streak of fierce independence running through Kiribati culture. Catholic or protestant, people were islanders first, and Jesus never said that the world wasn't made of turtles. Culture gets overridden, but there are deeper things than a person's religion.

---

[5] I also learned that this story is not quite true. It is, in fact, a version of one told by Stephen Hawking about Bertrand Russel in his book *A Brief History of Time*. The original quote reads:

A well-known scientist (some say it was Bertrand Russell*) once gave a public lecture on astronomy. He described how the earth orbits around the sun and how the sun, in turn, orbits around the center of a vast collection of stars called our galaxy. At the end of the lecture, a little old lady at the back of the room got up and said: "What you have told us is rubbish. The world is really a flat plate supported on the back of a giant tortoise." The scientist gave a superior smile before replying, "What is the tortoise standing on?" "You're very clever, young man, very clever," said the old lady. "But it's turtles all the way down!"*

At the time, I was unaware of this quotation having never read Hawking, and the intrepid and well-read I-Kiribati priest who told me this tale presented it as having taken place on Abaiang.

Once I heard a story about a Catholic missionary who was having a theological discussion with one of the local men from Abaiang.

"The world cannot possibly rest on the backs of turtles," he argued. "What would the turtles rest on?"

"Turtles," replied the villager. "It's turtles all the way down."[5]

*　　　*　　　*

To be in Kiribati is to be dependent on the sea. People believed in turtles because they were there, surrounding them, circulating in the waters near the islands like blood cells. They could be seen and touched and so what if a few were harvested to feed the village? There was never a shortage. A foreign God cannot replace that sort of abundance.

Kiribati had an immensity of turtles, an effusion of turtles, an economy of turtles. In the end, how different is that from an economy based on money? At least turtles actually exist.

*　　　*　　　*

Touch

We made the same salaries as native teachers. It ended up being a few hundred Australian dollars a month. We used our money to buy food. The rest we saved. There were few living expenses on the island. Our house was provided for us. It was made of coconut sticks and pandanus. Our water came from a well near our house. Our electricity came from a neighbor's solar panel. It powered one light. Most I-Kiribati teachers have large families to support, kids, spouses, brothers and sister, mothers and fathers, cousins and even friends sometimes live with each other on one income. We had no such obligations. By the standards of the village, Raven and I were rich.

The money didn't matter. We had trouble getting fish. I'm not a fisherman and we lived in a village of teachers. Fish was scarce. In other villages, the men spent all day fishing, and their families ate well. We ate rice and canned beans that we bought in bulk and had shipped to us from the capital island, Tarawa.

*   *   *

When we got back to America, the Peace Corps gave us 10,000 dollars as a readjustment allowance. We bought a truck, and the money vanished. I am happy with the purchase. It is a good truck. It runs well. It hauls our other stuff from place to place, holds most of our possessions, but it is not part of us, and we are not a part of it. When it's gone, I will not pine for it. I will buy a new truck. This is how it works. We buy things and discard them. The world becomes disposable.

*   *   *

When you fly over Kiribati, it looks like hundreds of green backs alive and writhing. From the sea, as the early Kiribati explorers must have seen them, the islands dome ever so slightly above the waves. As you approach, the boat slides through the troughs and crests, the view of the land, alternating between the barest edge of green and glimpses of reddish coral and dense jungle. Most of the islands are roughly circular or oval, the interior being the lagoon. The land, itself, is a thin ribbon, no more than a half mile wide at the widest and mostly thinner. Villages are carved out of the bush, reclaimed in brown swaths that stretch from ocean to lagoon like scars. Who could blame the ancient islanders for thinking of turtles at first sight?

*   *   *

I thought of turtles at the Spiral Jetty, a land art installation on the northern shore of the Great Salt Lake which stretches out into the water in a long coil of earth and rock. I was out there with friends. We'd come to have a look at the land, having heard that there were plans in the works to drill for oil in the lake near there. The road down to the jetty is dusty and long and as it nears the edge of the Great Salt Lake, it begins to look more like a boulder field than a road. We parked the car and hiked the last quarter mile carrying a large round piece of plywood made to look like the Earth.

The plywood was part of an art project we had undertaken. Coins and paper money of different nationalities made up the ocean and the land. An Earth made of money. Our idea was to juxtapose this with the Jetty, to have one piece of art comment on another.

We walked the spiral to the center, and spent time on the flat, hard ground at the edge of the water wondering at the salt encrusted bodies of hundreds of grasshoppers. How did they come to be here? How did they die? We walked out across the salt. The water, forming only the thinnest film over the crystals, made it seem like ice and we worried we would break through and fall into the saline water of the lake. It held us, however, and we spread our arms and pretended we were walking on water, Christ-like, blasphemous. The pose, belying intention, for this trip was meant as a sort of redemption, a way to save ourselves, though we were not sure of how or from what.

One of the photos we took holds particular significance for me. A girl from our group is crouching behind the Earth, propping it up without letting herself be seen. The shot is from the side and shows her, head down, reflected in the shallow water, the plywood leaning against her. The world

Touch

rests upon her and she is crouched down on a rim of protruding salt. I hear it crunch beneath her feet as she adjusts, shifts her weight to accommodate that of the Earth. It is an exchange of sorts, a dependence. There is so much salt, mountains of it, lakefuls, huge underground caverns of it. The rime of it is on my skin, the taste of it in my mouth, bitter and chalky and salty. And beneath that: salt. And beneath that: salt. And beneath that…

My friend Lindsy had brought her daughter and she tried, over and over again to rush into the lake, towards the very heart of it, Lindsy sprinting after her, her voice rising higher the farther they went. I remember thinking she was moving in the right direction. We'd come to connect with the landscape, and here we all were, at the edges while Coral sprinted towards the water.

I imagined the salt, domed below us like the back of some monstrous salt turtle, its other side buried beneath the alkaline soil of Abaiang. The places, connected by what is underneath.

We should've lain down on the rime,
should've rolled over and over, steeped ourselves in
it. We should've rushed into the water and
submerged, should've baptized ourselves in salt,
paid homage to the god of real things.

* * *

I am terrified of getting this wrong. My
god, destruction is so easy, so natural. My son is
the size of a raspberry, fragile inside of my fragile
wife. I am tiptoeing around her, touching only with
great care, blowing gently on the heart of the
flames. Every nerve in my body jangles.

If only it were true, if I could believe in
turtles, that as the sea rises, Kiribati will simply
float instead of being drowned. If only the world
could swim away and save itself.

Some part of me knows that all this worry is
futile, that more people is always a bad idea, that
there is no surer way to find destruction than by
creating, and yet, I'm doing my mad, voodoo dance,
limbs crossed, eyes closed, covered in talismans and

Touch

rabbits feet, chanting ancient charms. "He will be different. This one will be different."

*   *   *

15th November 2010

Dear Ezra,

I want you to be happy. I'll begin there. I could say that I want you to go to a good school or to get straight A's or to be a great writer, but that would be dishonest. I want you to be satisfied with whatever your life turns out to be. I can't help thinking that a decent education is part of what will shape you. I expect that you will have enough money. I need you to be safe. I won't say that you should live in a huge house in the suburbs, but I admit I've thought about it. It seems safe and prosperous to settle down and make sure that you become well adjusted.

On the other hand, it's unlikely that you will get to touch a baby sea turtle in a suburb in the Midwest.

I'm torn. I want to protect you from the risks I see out there in the world. It's a dangerous world.

But I want you to find some way to make contact, too. I'm not sure there's a way to do both. In fact, I'm sure that the kind of safety I am, right now, imagining is an illusion. More people die in car accidents than bear attacks. More people are murdered in the suburbs than are struck by lightning on mountain tops.

Somehow it seems safer, though, to stay out of sight. I'm drawn to the hiding places, to the insides of buildings with air conditioning and heat and running water and soft beds, but I know there are things underneath of that world. I know there is a living, breathing beast of a something below us, and whatever that is, turtle or God, it can see through our flimsy walls, can see us for what we are. We are a species of Earth. The old legends say that we are born of it, of dust and clay and breath, and to that we shall return. We cannot hide.

Touch

Your mother and I love you. More than that, to us you are all that exists. You are our salt, our turtle.

We are proud of you, though you are only the size of raspberry now. Last night we sang to you and I wanted to let you sleep next to my old blanket so you wouldn't be scared, but your mother said it would be too silly to sleep with such an old and worn bit of cotton on her belly.

We are trying to be good for you. We are trying to be better than we are.

FOR EZRA

One day you will ask me where you came from. And I will answer:

You were born out of pure terror. You were born out of desperation, in the middle of the night, out of a strangling tightness that was killing us. You were born in darkness and your mother and I clung to each other in the gloaming and we could not get close enough... so we had you.

You were born in violence, of split lips and black eyes and bruises. In an attempt to escape from a world gone mad, you were born in madness.

You were a last ditch effort, a Hail Mary, a cry in the dark. You are made of the flesh and bones of the Earth and we cobbled you together without knowing exactly what we were doing, what we might unleash.

You were a frightening possibility, all arms and legs and potential and we put you together because we needed something more than just each other and the dying Earth.

You were born from an Earth shattering stillness, in desperation and hope, and hope is a terrible thing.

You were born a thing of teeth and claws all hardness and piercing agony. You were born of screams and yells and pleas and ragged breath. You were born and you saved our lives. You were born and you protected us. You were born and your naked pink body, the very softness of you was a shield for us. You were born invincible and courageous. You were born to outlive us. We hold you up as a talisman against the world. We hold you up as a cross and a sign, as a miracle. Behold this child who has brought us out of ruin and decay!

You are beautiful and terrible and you come out of our love which is beautiful and terrible, and out of the Earth which is beautiful and terrible and so you see how your beauty and terror are a spire, a light out of the waste.

You are born of hope and hope is the thing with feathers and the thing with talons and the thing with teeth and the thing with a thousand arms so we can hold you tight tight tight tight tight! You are our baby, our son, our child and weloveyouweloveyouweloveyou.

IN DARKNESS

Three days without sleep. We toss and turn together, and there's lightning in the mountains, bright flashes that light the dark. I could count the number of times I've seen a thunderstorm in Salt Lake on one hand until now. It's a sea change. The whole state used to be in the middle of a huge, saline lake and I feel like it's poised to return.

Raven is sick, has been for weeks now. It is this baby, this child in her belly, like an alien force. A power we've managed to conceive but not control. She can't stand up, can't eat. "It reminds me of dengue fever," she says. "It's been so long since I felt well."

I remember the fever. She came down with it a month or so before we left our village for good.

Dengue fever is also called break bone fever. It is one of the tropical diseases predicted to migrate north as the climate shifts. Victims feel searing bone pain and crushing fatigue and nausea. She was sick for almost three weeks with it in

August of 2006. The fever is caused by a virus
transmitted through mosquito bites. Supposedly,
only one kind of mosquito carries the virus noted
because the species bites only in daylight. We got
this information from our medical officer, a
competent P.A. with years of experience dealing
with tropical diseases. The information was all she
could give us. The fever, she said, had to run its
course. Raven rode out the worst of the sickness in
the sweltering heat on our buia[6] in the middle of the
jungle. She slept and sweated and shivered through
it and there was no relief, no cold shower, no air
conditioning or chicken soup. I talked to her, did
what I could, but really, there was no helping. I felt
powerless... like now.

Not long before the fever began, we climbed
the highest building on our island. It was a church
and it was made of bricks and mortar four stories
high. The soil of Abaiang cannot have been
suitable for brick-making, so the bricks must have
been imported. In fact, everything from the stained

---

[6] A buia is a raised platform made of sticks with a thatched
roof and no sides.

glass windows to the cross on the steeple, to Catholicism itself was imported, put here on a sandy atoll in the middle of nowhere for what purpose?

There was even a clock tower though it had stopped working long ago. A remnant from a misguided attempt to impose hours and minutes on the land and its inhabitants.

The route to the top of the tower was dangerous. It consisted of rickety old ladders with missing rungs and they bent and swung under our weight as we climbed. I was sure we would come crashing down at any moment. The tallest palm trees on the island might have been fifty feet high and we were above them by the time we'd finished climbing the third ladder. A hundred feet, a hundred and fifty, and we were on the roof, finally basking in the cool breeze. Our tour guide was an old Catholic priest. He stood with us and told us of the first missionaries who came to Abaiang in the 1800s. I wondered that he chose to begin his tales there.

Even then, the island was full up with
people, as many villagers as the land and sea could
support. The missionaries translated the bible into
Kiribati, built this church, told everyone they'd
have to start wearing clothes and then left, mostly,
for more exciting destinations with richer natural
resource reserves.

We looked down the length of the island. It
was not the same as seeing it from the window of a
plane. There was no pane of shatter proof glass
between us and the wind. The tower seemed to
sway in the breeze, and we could smell the ocean,
fresh and clear. Our village, our schools, our house
spread out below us in one long green/brown line
was almost indistinguishable from the surrounding
trees. All of these familiar things were so small and
the ocean... I'd never seen anything so huge. It
went on as far as we could see. Only a hint of cloud
on the horizon told us there might be another island
out there, just beyond our vision. This, I thought, is
where history should begin, with the hint of some
unknowable mystery drawing us on.

Touch

I remember wondering how the island could have stood here so long, this tiny speck of land in the middle of all that blue. It seemed as though one good wave would have wiped it off the face of the Earth.

*   *   *

Kiribati has survived contact with Europeans largely intact. There have been losses. Kiribati lore, legends about the creation of the world, stories from before colonization have largely disappeared or are in the process of disappearing. Fishing has modernized. Spears have been replaced with spear guns and nets are now made with plastic instead of coconut fiber. Motorbikes and trucks have made their way out to the islands, but overall, Kiribati is still a nation of fisherman and toddy[7] cutters rather than factory workers. The country has been spared because its islands are small and remote. Its only natural resource is phosphate and though there are mining operations on some atolls, for the most part, the islands are so remote as to

---

[7] Toddy is coconut palm sap. It is a sweet syrup that can be drunk plain or used to flavor food.

make mineral extraction unprofitable. The very features of Kiribati that make it so harsh and unattractive to Europeans and Americans have been the saving grace of the country.

In every sense of the word, the I-Kiribati[8] are survivors. They've lived on their islands for thousands of years under conditions most Westerners would consider unlivable, and they've built a thriving culture. The unforgiving sea and the harsh equatorial sun could not dislodge them. An invasion of I-Matangs[9] could not destroy their culture. Now, the country sits precariously on the brink of annihilation. We've teamed up, Westerners and the sun and the sea: climate change. I guess we'll see what happens.

*   *   *

---

[8] I-Kiribati refers to a person from Kiribati. The prefix I- attached to a place refers to the people who live in that place. Hence the word for a white person is I-Matang which refers to a mythical land from Kiribati legend inhabited by people with pale skin.
[9] I-Matangs are any foreigner or outsider, usually a person with white skin. The term comes from a Kiribati legend about an island across the sea inhabited with pale skinned people who are sometimes characterized as ghosts.

The Saturday we found out we were pregnant, she woke up crying. There was blood. We were certain that she had started her period, and devastated to find out that our experiment hadn't worked. I comforted her as best I could, but there was a feeling of defeat in the air as we ate breakfast and planned out the day.

We bought wine. We hadn't been drinking while we tried to get pregnant, sure that we were moments away from conception and wanting to be as cautious as possible. Now, however, we recklessly bought two bottles, a red and a white, intending to drink them before we tried again.

It is a strange thing after years of care, of precaution against pregnancy, attention to the details of bodily fluids exchange, to suddenly throw out the birth control and have the most dangerous sex, to risk pregnancy, to hope for it even. There is something freeing in that prospect, and we took up the torch enthusiastically. Some days we had sex two and three times, basking in the glory of our reproductive potential, all the while conscious of how this might end.

We felt rebellious, free, like we were the first people on Earth making some new discovery about the nature of life. It was like the first day in a foreign country. Your eyes open wider, your senses come alive, you notice the details of your surroundings, the different greens, the novel kinds of foliage, the smell of low tide, pungent and sharp in the nostrils, the sounds of crashing waves. All of this combined with the already heady sensations of sex. No wonder we were disappointed that our foray into unexplored territory came up empty.

Just before we opened the wine, she decided to take a pregnancy test… to be sure. She peed on the stick and set it aside and we both went into different rooms to wait out the three minutes it takes for potential results. After two minutes, I sneaked back and looked and saw a faint line where a positive result would appear. I sneaked back out of the room, my mind a haze of excitement and confusion. I didn't dare tell Raven lest the line

Touch

disappear in the intervening minute before we read the test. I waited in the bathroom as my legs and arms began to lose feeling. My knees felt weak. My breathing was shallow. I struggled to get a grip on myself. Was this terror or elation?

Whatever it was, I was woefully unprepared. Finally, I heard Raven's voice from the bedroom. "Come here and look at this." It was urgent and dire. There was a gravity to the situation that I could not have fully grasped before, and as I made my way to the bedroom, time itself seemed to slow. I remember the look on her face, the same one she wore when she'd found out that our bank statement was in negative figures, the same one she wore when we found out that our nephew, born extremely premature, had died.

We both examined the test for several seconds and then I told her I thought she was pregnant and we held each other tight and cried. The wine we'd bought would have to be given away. We were pregnant. There was the beginning of a baby inside my wife, growing at that moment, growing persistently as he is at this very moment, as he will be for years and years until we are old and he is an adult. Even now, when I think of it, it takes my breath away knowing that I am a father, that I will hold my son in my arms in April, that my life has changed and cannot be changed back.

*   *   *

One day, we were biking to the council station near the center of our island to mail a letter, and when we got there, all we found was blood. There was a pool of it on the cement floor near the front steps and it was spattered all over the walls as if someone had been beaten to death. None of the workers who tended the station were there. It was as though everyone had disappeared. And then we saw the tracks. They were human tracks, barefoot, and the person who'd made them had either walked through the blood or had been the one doing the bleeding. We followed them through the low cinder block building and then out the back door. They went down towards the road, so we went back for our bikes and followed. At the road, they turned

left, away from our village. We rode slowly over
the gravel and the prints kept going, leading us on.
Sometimes we saw circles or spatters of blood
where the bleeding person must have stopped for a
moment. We guessed that he or she was still
bleeding freely because sometimes the spots were
as large as dinner plates. At one point, the footsteps
faded, but the blood trail continued in drips and
splatters a quarter mile, a half mile, a mile. There
was an airstrip down this way, another mile or so.
We thought the injured person might be headed
there to get on a flight and get to a real hospital.
We rode faster, fearing that he or she was still
walking, even now. That she might need help.

And then the drips stopped. There were no
other tracks, no footprints or tire tracks, no sign of
anyone, no sign of a body. They were just gone.
We looked up the road another quarter mile. We
looked down a side road that led to a Catholic
school. Nothing. Eventually we turned back and
rode home to our village without stopping, without
even finding someone to mail our letter. What had

happened? Had he died? Had she been rescued by
someone and taken to a nurse? We never found out.

I worry about it sometimes, about who had
bled so much, and then disappeared. In the U.S. we
could have tuned into the news and found out who it
was and how it happened. Perhaps someone with a
video phone might have caught the whole accident
on tape. Here, there was no news except what
filtered through the bush to our village and on the
subject of the bloody trail in the road, silence.

Perhaps we should have looked harder, tried
harder to find out, to help. The image of the blood
disturbs me. I don't want to imagine it stretched out
like that all over the road. How much was it? a
pint? a quart? How much can a person lose and
live?

*   *   *

I've seen pictures of the oil spill in the Gulf,
the Macando blowout, the oil reddish brown and
spread across the ocean like a sheen of new paint. I
cannot wrap my arms around it, cannot grasp it.
How much is it? Where has it come from? Is it the

Touch

blood of the Earth, the marrow, from deep within its bones? I look at it and I understand that this is only a fraction of the whole. In a few months it will be out of sight and out of mind for most of us, vanished into the ether.

I can't help thinking that the Earth is meant to devour us. That's what oil is, anyway. It's us, decayed and rotten and chemically altered under heat and pressure, but us. Crack crack slurp. We suck out the marrow, clean the bones, cannibals.

This oil is killing us. The spill is a calamity, but it's not the whole story, just the most visible part of it. The oil I don't see, the stuff that gets refined and burned and pushed out of tailpipe and exhaust ports, the stuff that hangs in the air over Salt Lake City and disperses and travels around the globe, the stuff that turns into carbon dioxide as it burns and then absorbs and emits solar radiation, the stuff that, little by little, is melting glaciers and disrupting climate patterns. There's so much of it, so much disaster. And we are so fragile, more vulnerable than anyone is willing to admit.

One good wave. We cannot ride this out.

I will have a child goddamnit! I will have a child and he will matter. He will be of the Earth, of me, of his mother, of our desires and fears, of our hope though it sometimes seems futile. I will have him and I will hold him in my arms and it will be different. It will be beautiful. The world will begin to make sense.

To me, he is an abundance, the overriding thing. I imagine him, green eyed and fierce. His face in profile is the bole of an aspen, his tiny hands, the roots of oleander. His hair is the soft ends of owl feathers. It's as if the world is made of him.

*   *   *

I am awake again, worried sick, the covers cloy and stick. It is hot. The darkness presses in, closes like hands upon me. I think of blood trails, of silky smooth waves. I can't put my mind on him, can't feel the exactness of skin to skin. He is inaccessible. I turn towards my sleeping wife and listen for a while to her long breaths. They are deep

Touch

and slow. I know that I could reach out, I imagine it; gently lifting the sheets and slowly, softly caressing her belly. I imagine the feel of pounding blood in my fingers, the heat of her bare skin, the tiny life within. I begin the slow process, the tiny movements, shifting my weight ever so carefully so as not to wake her. My hand hovers over her and I pause. I can feel it, the radiant heat, the slow fire. He is here. He is here. I repeat it over and over again like a mantra, convincing myself of the facts. Slowly, slowly, I lower my hand and stretch out along my side. She moves in her sleep, contracting in towards the warmth of my body, and slowly, slowly, I relax. The soft skin of her belly rests under my fingers and below that, my son lies curled, heart beating.

ENOUGH

Long, long ago, there was Nareau. Nareau means 'the spider'. He was a god, but a god who could do human things. No one knew his origin, from where he was, or who his parents were. He was floating in space all alone, sleeping.

While he was floating, he dreamt that somebody called his name, "Nareau, why do you lie like that doing nothing?" Nareau was very surprised to hear somebody call his name. He opened his eyes to see who it was. He could not see anyone. There was nobody there. His name was called yet again, for the third time. He began to realize that there was no one calling his name but that it was just a dream. When he woke the third time, he began to stretch his arms and legs and yawn and sneeze.

He then said, "Who calls my name?" Nobody answered, for he was alone and no one else was there. He began to look around. He saw nothing but emptiness. When he looked down, he saw a sealed object floating below him. It was *Te Bomatemaki* (The Earth and Sky Sealed Together).

When Nareau the Creator saw *Te Bomatemaki* floating far below he was very curious about it, and to satisfy his curiosity he descended and stood on it and looked at it carefully. He thought of opening it to see what it was like inside.

Taking his tail called *Kaweten bukin Nareau (The Barb of the Spider),* he walked about on *Te*

Bomatemaki with his tail, first to the north and chanted:

"I stamp, I stamp,
Over the skies to the northward;
There are neither spirits nor men;
But only I,
The Powerful Nareau."

He repeated the same process till he had completed four rounds in *Te Bomatemaki,* first to the north, then to the south, to the east and to the west. When he had done this he noticed that nothing had happened. There was neither a crack nor an opening on the surface of *Te Bomatemaki.* He thought again, and eventually tried to slit it open. He crouched down and started to slit *Te Bomatemaki* with his tail, while chanting these words:

"Dense, dense, rock, rock,
Crack of what? Crack of rock,
Crack of what? Crack of boulder,
It is I, the Powerful Nareau
Oh! Let it crack."

He repeated the same process three times. As a result, a crack appeared on *Te Bomatemaki,* and he forced it open.

– from *Kiribati: Aspects of History*

Sometimes belief in climate change seems like a religion. This is how the cosmology works out.

There is almighty carbon, the holy trinity of oil, gas, and coal.

Releasing too much CO_2 shall bring down terrible wrath upon us.

The sun shall shine down on us with great power. The deserts shall be converted to a furnace. The wetlands shall be deluged. The polar ice caps shall melt and release a flood to drown the seaside sinners and their valuable real-estate.

To avoid these things, I adhere to certain practices. I bike to work. I grow as much of my own food as possible. I set the thermostat as low as I can stand.

These acts have ritual significance. They are sacraments, holy in their own right with no reason behind them. I do these things and they are good.

I think of it this way because climate change is still, mostly, unreal to me. There is Kiribati, of course, the fact that it is soon to be underwater, but proof is about numbers, facts, concrete assertions that can be tested.

Touch

The scientific arguments in favor of climate change make sense as far as I can follow them. I took physics in high school and I remember the laws of thermodynamics and how systems function, but I'm not a real scientist. Most Americans aren't, and all that's left is to trust our own eyes.

The problem is that the Earth still seems, for the most part, immense and unblemished.

I look out my window at the Wasatch Mountains, and I do not see degradation. The mountains are beautiful in the light of early evening, tinged with an orange glow and imposing. It seems that they have always been there, will always be there. How can I believe the world is going to hell?

I heard a radio story on NPR not long ago. In it, a reporter interviewed several I-Kiribati. He asked whether they believed their islands were going underwater.

"Climate change is an all natural phenomenon. You can't really do much about that, unless you can talk to God and negotiate with

God…. He made a promise to Noah that he will never again destroy this earth with flood. (Reed)"

I want to believe it. I want Kiribati to be spared, but if there is a god, I'm not convinced she is watching us.

Nature has never been benevolent. Despite the religious fervor of human beings, there have always been hurricanes, tornadoes, earthquakes, tsunamis, eruptions, wildfires, cave-ins, floods, famines, freezes, heat waves, sandstorms, and other disasters. Even in the absence of disaster, the Earth is not exactly a hospitable place. Temperatures rise and fall. Snow, rain, and hail fall from the sky. Edible plants die off in winter and sometimes refuse to return in spring. It takes an enormous effort just to stay alive. If you've ever gone backpacking, you already know all this. The Earth is a harsh place. The idea of colossal disaster fits right in with this profile.

Most climate activists suggest that, at some point, climate change will become apocalyptic on a societal scale. Governments will be unable to cope with the massive disruptions to their food and fuel supplies and chaos will ensue.

The most optimistic activists predict that the climate crisis will bring out our best natures, that we will adapt, learn to live within our means. We will grow our own food, locally. We will give up consumer culture and conspicuous consumption. We will govern ourselves by consensus in small, independent communities. Peace will prevail.

Others take a darker view of the aftermath of such devastation. When they look to the future, they see Warlords with gangs of violent men, raping and pillaging their way across the country, trying to scrape the last of the Earth's resources from the bottom of the barrel.

I believe that if such a crisis occurs, we will fall somewhere in the middle. Both our best and worst natures will come to the fore. We will relearn local lore, create small communities, and live more sustainably because we will be forced to, but we will also resurrect the ancient prejudices and superstitions inherent to tribal culture. The strange primitive magic which dwells within us, and which we cannot leave behind.

Ironically, the same crisis that threatens to devour Kiribati, may eventually spawn new societies more similar to pre-contact Kiribati than to the U.S. as we now know it.

I don't know how to prepare, how to prepare my son.

I've thought about buying a farm and bunch of guns, of storing years worth of canned goods and dried food, of putting up barbed wire, of stockpiling gasoline and diesel fuel. I've thought about putting up solar panels and wind turbines, of drilling a deep well so that our compound will have a supply of fresh water. I've thought of leaving society, of homeschooling Ezra and keeping him away from harmful influences. The more I think about it, the less I believe it is the answer.

Climate change is an all natural phenomenon, but it has been brought about by one species of organism that lives on the planet. In the same way a bloom of algae can change the pH of a lake and kill off all the other organisms that live in it, human beings have the potential to disrupt the fundamental chemistry behind the Earth's natural systems. We are animals. We are ruled, not by any rational set of principles, but by instinct, and sometimes, instinct fails.

Whether or not there is a crisis brewing, whether or not we have an obligation to reverse it, whether or not God exists... my own actions are beyond such trivialities.

I walk to work because it is not far from my house. I grow vegetables because they taste good, and it gives me joy to pick green beans and eat them. If my wife says she's cold, I adjust the heat regardless of my belief in climate change.

My life is moment by moment. It is sometimes shaped by my choices and other times, it is beyond my control. If God exists, she finds expression in the details, the unexpected.

I notice, however, that I find myself in the presence of a kinder god most often when I think of Kiribati and those people I knew there, or of Raven or Ezra, my family and friends, of wildflowers blooming near an alpine lake in Maine or a lonely black bear whose tail I saw disappearing into the woods in New Hampshire or a family of short eared owls in a marsh in Montana. The awareness of these things brings forth my most tender impulses: compassion, empathy, altruism. The decisions I make from the heart of love, from this gentleness require sacrifice, letting go. Surely I use more than my fair share of resources, more gas and food and water and oil than I need, but each decision I make has the potential to bring me closer to where I know I should be, which is closer to zero, to no impact to a better life for my son.

What can I do without so that he will have enough? This is the question I find myself asking. It lies near the heart of the ethical dilemma of ecology. As human beings, what is our responsibility to each other, and what is our responsibility to the rest of the beings on the planet?

It is the awareness of this question, the awareness of the needs of others, of the connections between us that allows me to believe in the kind of future my son and his son and his son ought to have. If those connections exist, if I am aware of them, then perhaps God becomes less relevant, and I can begin to have faith in something else.

I believe in melting ice caps, in polar bears stranded at sea, in thawing permafrost.

I believe in rising sea levels, in feedback loops, and disrupted bird migrations.

I believe in the northward movement of tropical disease, in larger, more powerful storms, and longer droughts.

I believe in these things though I've never seen them. I believe they are evidence of climate change. I believe they are drawing closer.

And I almost believe in destruction, that somehow it may be easier to simply concede, to let go the things I love in the hope that without human beings the earth might begin to heal. Perhaps we deserve as much, to be wiped out as a result of our own carelessness and stupidity.

There are depths of cruelty within me, and greed and fear and apathy. There is corruption and exploitation and all manner of evil, but perhaps there are good things too, beauty and love and peace, and I am trying to be guided by my best impulses.

May it be enough.

TITO

We will stand before whoever is able and willing to
judge, or perhaps the silence of extinction, as a
generation that willfully and unnecessarily imposed
egregious wrongs on all future generations,
depriving them of liberty, property, and life.
      –David Orr

I am continually given strange advice when
I go to talks on climate change. Most of these are
replete with graphs and tables, pictures or live video
of melting glaciers, and at least one shot of a polar
bear that seems to have been thrown in almost as an
afterthought. Then there is the hopeful, upbeat slide
near the end of the presentation where the presenter
throws out easy, everyday solutions, things all of us
can do right now to start saving the planet. Change
from incandescent to compact fluorescent light
bulbs. Drive less. Grow your own food. Install
solar panels on the roof of your house.

A friend of mine told me about one
conference he'd gone to where the presenter
skipped this part. Afterwards, he asked her about it.

"You didn't say what we can do about climate change." She put her hand on his shoulder and he said there was a deep sadness in her eyes.

"I'm sorry," she said. "My generation failed yours."

There is no solution to climate change, no scenario in which we avoid the two degree rise in global average temperature, none in which polar bears survive, or the ice cap doesn't melt to almost nothing. Even the most optimistic projections I've heard, the ones that assume huge reductions in greenhouse gasses and a stable global population within a few decades, note that it is too late to avoid the lion's share of effects. This is because of the long term feedback loops associated with climate change. Increases in atmospheric CO_2 do not immediately result in higher average temperatures. It can take twenty-five years for that to happen, but even if there weren't feedback loops, even if it was as simple and straightforward as possible, we stop polluting today and in a month, everything is back to normal... could we stop? stop using our cars?

stop turning on our lights? stop pumping our world full of poison?

These things are like tiger tracks, proof of…?

I think there is a kind of curiosity to it. We need to see how far this will go. Perhaps it is the roots of a pervasive death wish, a pornographic urge towards misery and destruction.

The name "climate change" gives a suggestion that the whole thing is benign. Perhaps it should be called that problem where we fucked the Earth up.

*   *   *

My shoes were stolen. This was years ago now and the shoes are long dead, but you remember stolen objects. I had a bike that was stolen my freshman year of college and I still look for it, though I am in a completely different city and ten years have passed. I plan on seeing the bike eventually, just as it was (though in truth I can't remember anymore what it looked like) with the thief mounted on it. I will rush up from behind and tackle him and take back what is mine.

This is unlikely to the point of madness, but I still fantasize about it whenever I think of that bike, and I tell myself that it was a beauty, too, the finest bike I ever owned.

I got the shoes back. I wonder, sometimes, how it would be if I hadn't. Probably exactly the same except that I'd be angrier about the whole thing and half-expecting to meet Tito walking out of a seedy bar in downtown Salt Lake, wearing them. As it is, I'm aware they're gone. I threw them away myself when one of the straps broke last year. Sometimes I feel a little bad about it. I've spent a lot of time and energy thinking about those shoes. That's what it feels like anyway, and they're not even around anymore.

*   *   *

While I was a volunteer, I attempted to coerce native peoples into speaking English and getting jobs, staying sober. I think this may have been a bad idea. I didn't drink much while I lived

Touch

in Ueen Wakaam. I had one or two at a time and then called it a night. I didn't drink Kava at all except for one time when my country director was there and wanted to try it. My intent was to show everyone that you can stop after one or two. You don't have to get shitfaced.

I was wrong.

Once, I asked one of the men about it.

"Why do you drink so much? Why do you stay up all night drinking kava?"

He looked at me for a long time and then he smiled and laughed.

"It is our culture," he said.

*   *   *

Raven and I were at the Australian embassy on Tarawa. Another volunteer we knew was dating an Australian diplomat and we had tagged along with her to a party. There were less than a dozen of us sitting at a long wooden table under a pavilion with a tin roof. It was raining off and on. We were at the end of the table and couldn't hear anything anyone was saying because of the noise of rain and tin colliding. This did not matter all that much as we didn't know anyone there except Whitney and she was wrapped tightly around her Australian lover at the other end of the table. We were drinking beer and wondering whether it would be impolite to leave in a few minutes, and then the rain stopped abruptly.

Tito was drunk when we met him. In fact, I never saw him again, so he was drunk one hundred percent of the time that I knew him.

"What's your name," he said to me. His English was rather good, only slightly accented though he slurred a little and his eyes went in and out of focus when he spoke.

I told him my name.

"Are you from Peace Corps then?"

"Yes." There was a look of approval at this. Peace Corps was respectable.

"What island?"

"Abaiang."

He shrieked. It was loud and long and so slurred that it took me a minute to realize it was a word, "Aaabaiaaaaaang."

"I'm from Abaiang," he said. There was a huge grin on his face now and I leaned towards him. Sharing an island is like being related. We could have been cousins.

"Are you?" I asked.

He wailed again, "Aaabaaaaiiiiaaaaaaaang." He paused for breath, took a swig of beer. He emptied the can and opened another. "I used to teach at Ueen Wakaam," he said.

"I teach there now." I was smiling. This was a coincidence indeed.

"Did you see the computers in the staff room there?" He didn't wait for an answer. "I got those." He nodded importantly. I was supposed to be impressed. I was impressed. There were three computers in the staffroom at my school, ancient things with rust all over them, but they worked well enough to make party invitations, typed ones with clip-art pictures printed on them, which I had received from time to time. Having working computers was no mean feat on an island with no electricity. Every time they were used, we had to fire up a generator in the next room. It was so loud and unpleasant that it was almost not worth the effort involved to type anything. He had reason to be proud.

We talked for a while longer about Abaiang and the teachers we both knew and then, with a last wail of AAAAbaiiiiiiiiaaaaaaaang, he left. Raven had barely spoken to him at all which wasn't that surprising. Kiribati men tended to speak to me and ignore her, but she was bored, and we decided to leave too. We said our goodbyes and walked to the end of the pavilion closest to the road before I noticed.

"Has anyone seen my shoes?" It was hard to get the group's attention. Everyone was pretty drunk and the rain had started again which was making conversation difficult. I looked all around the deck and then I widened the search to the lawn, the various outbuildings. I even looked in the pool to see if someone had thrown them in as a joke, but they were gone. I walked back to the pavilion, wet and a little pissed off.

"Hey, have any of you seen my shoes?" This time I got their attention.

"Your shoes?" Most of the Australians at the table looked puzzled.

"I'll bet Tito took them." The speaker was a skinny kid about halfway down the table. He was half Kiribati judging from his skin tone. Probably half Australian or Kiwi by his accent.

"Where did he go?"

"The Royal, I think."

The Royal was a nightclub in Betio. I had never been, but a friend of mine had once gotten punched in the face when he'd walked into a bar fight there. I didn't know the way.

*　　　*　　　*

The evidence in support of climate change is solid. Because of human beings and our carbon emissions, the world is changing for the worse. I've seen most of this evidence in one form or another, but it's foreign to me. I cannot translate it into anything meaningful.

What's the difference between 250 and 350 parts per million CO_2? How will I know when fifty percent of the biodiversity on the planet has disappeared? These numbers mean very little to me, and though I know better, my instinct is to let someone else worry about it.

I am waiting for disaster, clear and obvious.

I feel it coming. Every harm I take part in, every bit of plastic I throw away, every time I get in the car and drive, every light switch I flip, every moment I stand under the hot water of my shower, every ounce of dish detergent I wash down the drain, every new thing I buy. They add up.

I remember as a child having to pick bagworms off of a pine tree and put them into a coffee can. There were so many, the tree seemed to be made of their soft brown cocoons. Soon after I started, I remember nearly crying because the job was so overwhelming. I couldn't imagine ever removing all of the worms. But after a few hours, I found myself picking the very last one from the tree. There must have been a thousand worms in the coffee can when I was done and my father set them on fire with some lighter fluid. I watched them writhe and squirm in the can as the fire converted them from organic matter to cinders.

Each of my harms, each sin against nature seems so small. The drip of gasoline I spill when filling up my car is miniscule compared to the Macondo well blowout, but these things add up. How long can the planet hold on? How many drips of gasoline does it take to overwhelm the system? No doubt, the number seems immense, but I know I can get there, one drop at a time. I am persistent and cruel.

And, of course, there are the shoes. They are, perhaps, the most compelling evidence of all. They were stolen and I got them back and it didn't even matter. Not even to me, and they were my shoes. Imagine… it wouldn't have mattered a lick if I'd never pursued them, except that Tito would have had an extra pair. I hate him for that.

I could not let them go.

*   *   *

"It's not far," said the half-caste. That was the term the Australians used to describe him, and it rang strangely true from behind the metal gates of the compound we were in. The buildings here were nothing special in terms of architecture, but they were solid and well kept in contrast to the rundown infrastructure typical of Tarawa. It was as if the compound were an early colonial fort meant to keep out troublemakers and riff-raff. Here was order. On the other side of the fence, all bets were off.

A few minutes later, we were on our way. It was raining harder now and we were both soaked to the skin. The streets of Betio were flooding and I was barefoot, slogging through the sudsy water.

"We should just go home," said Raven. She was tired and cold. I was too, but I told myself that aside from having lost my best shoes, this was a matter of principle. You can't just let people take your shoes. I had never met Tito before tonight and

I was pretty sure that I would never see him again if I didn't find him now.

"It's only a little farther," I said. We trudged on.

A few minutes later a truck pulled up beside us. We opened the door to find the half-caste inside.

"You want a lift?" It turned out that Tito had also taken his keys. He seemed resigned to it, as though this were the sort of thing that happened every night. Perhaps it did. We drove on a short while and came, finally, to The Royal. Loud music was blasting through the front door. A bouncer stepped in front of us as we drew near.

"Five dollars," he said.

"I'm just going in for a minute to talk to someone."

"Five dollars." He looked surly but also confused. I could tell his English was not very good.

"I'm just going to get my shoes." I was shouting to be heard over the music and pointing at my bare feet. The bouncer shook his head, but he moved aside and I went in. There were only three people in the club and one of them was the bartender. The walls were bland, unpainted plywood. Most nights it would be sweltering inside, but the rain had cooled everything down so that it was pleasant, though perhaps a bit claustrophobic due to the lack of windows. Tito was in a corner near the door talking to the only other patron and drinking yet another beer. I looked at his feet. He was not wearing my shoes.

*   *   *

Is it necessary to feel guilty about consumption? Aren't I allowed to buy my wife a Whopper when she craves meat? If I've had a hard day, don't I deserve to unwind with a pint of beer and another pint of Ben and Jerry's? Food is a necessity.

Raven and I have been discussing buying a new and bigger car. Should it be an SUV to keep our son safe? I am certainly entitled to keep Ezra as safe as I can, obligated even. I am entitled to own a

Suburban if I want one, and a Glock 19 in the name of safety, of peace of mind. They are needs, not wants.

Here is my advice for those seeking to avoid disaster:

Do not change light bulbs. Do not buy a Prius. If you must have an alternative vehicle, try a horse or a bicycle. Turn off your lights, but do this as you leave your house to go to the woods, or mountains, or desert. Go alone or with someone you love.

Walk through these places slowly. Do not wear insect repellant. Do not wear sunscreen. Walk in one direction until you can walk no more and then sit or lie down and wait until your mind is a blank and the wildness within you touches the wildness outside. Find out what is enough.

*   *   *

"Tito," I yelled. No reaction. I tapped him on the shoulder. He turned, blurry, red eyes trying hard to focus.

"Did you take my shoes?" I yelled. He was still staring apparently at a loss as to who I could be.

"Abaiiiiaaaaang," I yelled. His face lit up and he took a half step back. He wailed the word again. My head was beginning to ache from the noise.

"Did you take my shoes?" I asked again. He looked surprised and then looked down at his own feet which I'd already noticed were not clad in my shoes. He looked up and his face was very serious now. He walked over towards the bar and I followed. The bartender came over and Tito spoke to him for a moment. He bent down behind the bar and retrieved a plastic grocery bag. Inside it were three beers, a set of keys, and my sandals.

I took them from the bag and put them on. Tito gave the bag back to the barman and I left. The half-caste was just making his way through the door.

Outside the rain was falling as hard as ever and as we made our way back towards the main road to flag down a bus, the floodwater, warmed by

Touch

the asphalt, flowed like an extremely dirty creek around my ankles. I tried to nurse my anger, my indignation that someone had stolen my things, but I was tired and cold and my wife had put her arm around me in the darkness. The rain finally let up, and we stood there, shivering in the still night air, and my anger could not stand. We were so far from home.

GENTLENESS

Mom: "I love you so much that if a tiger walked
into the room right now, I'd let him eat me so you
could run away."
Me: "I love you so much that if a tiger came in the
room, I'd let him eat Dad."
> –Conversation between my mother and me
> circa 1986

Do not go gentle into that good night.
> –Dylan Thomas

1.

Shortly before Raven and I left for the Peace
Corps, we quit our jobs at a ski resort where we'd
been working in the childcare center. Along with
our final paychecks, we were given performance
evaluations. Mine enthusiastically praised my
attitude and work ethic and invited me to reapply at
any time in the future because they would love to
have me back. Raven's was slightly less glowing.

Despite working harder than I did, showing
up earlier, leaving later, and generally doing a better
job, her evaluation said that any future applications

she filled out would have to be reviewed most thoroughly and that she would have to demonstrate an improvement in her attitude if the resort was to rehire her.

The reason for this discrepancy had a lot to do with our boss in the childcare center. One night after work, she invited me and another employee out to a bar. We had a few drinks and somehow she ended up offering to buy us some cocaine "or mushrooms or acid… whatever you want. Just don't use it at work." I was shocked. I told Rebecca I had to go home and we never talked about drugs again, but I did tell the story to Raven, and from that point on, her attitude towards our boss changed.

Neither Raven nor I could bear the thought that our boss got high every weekend, that she was possibly addicted to cocaine. It was dangerous, and it was the sort of thing that ought to have disqualified her from any job working with kids. We didn't confront her about it, but we did agree to watch her closely for signs she was high at work. I managed to keep relations between Rebecca and myself fairly normal, but Raven has always been less adept at hiding her displeasure. She became colder toward our boss, and Rebecca couldn't help but pick up on her body language and her icy demeanor. Between the two of them, a bitter enmity took root. Raven's evaluation was the last shot in the war.

"That bitch," she said when she saw the evaluation. "I worked just as hard as you at that job. Probably harder."

"What's wrong?" My mom had overheard. We were living at my parents' house at the time which meant we'd made some compromises with regard to our privacy.

"It's nothing," said Raven. I could tell she didn't want to get into it.

"Are you sure?" My mom looked a little too concerned. I tried to set her at ease.

"It's just these stupid work evaluations. It's not like we'll ever go back and work at that resort again and it's not like Raven is going to put Rebecca down as a reference when she tries for a job after Peace Corps." My mother turned to face Raven, a sympathetic expression on her face.

"Did you get a bad evaluation?" she asked.

"It's not a big deal," said Raven.

"Do you need me to call over there and yell at someone?"

"Please don't," I said.

"Because I would."

"That's okay," said Raven.

"Alright, but I hate the idea of someone making my

feel bad." She hugged Raven before leaving the room.

We rolled our eyes. This sort of insistence on defending her children is one of the defining characteristics of my mother's personality. She can be fierce about it, calling up teachers or principals or coaches and giving them a piece of her mind. She is an intelligent and articulate woman, intimidating, though she is only five foot two.

She has bullied doctors into writing her prescriptions when they wanted to wait and see. She has scared sales associates into full cash refunds despite store policies. She has intimidated teachers into fearful apologies. She is the writer of angry letters, the unreasonable end of the kind of phone calls managers dread. Her wrath is both awe inspiring and infinitely embarrassing to my sister and I, and more recently to Raven. When she offers to go to bat for us, we always refuse and recant.

"It wasn't that bad," we say. "Actually, it was probably my fault." or "Please DO NOT CALL my professor. I am an adult." Anything to get her to back down.

A week after quitting our jobs, Raven and I were in Kiribati, and neither of us had given the issue at the ski resort another thought. We did not think about it, in fact, until around Christmas. We were in Australia visiting some friends and making phone calls to people back home because international calls from Australia are about fifty times cheaper than calls from Kiribati.

Touch

After I wished everyone Merry Christmas and got a rundown of the important news from the last six months, my mother and I reminisced for a while about the previous Christmas. I'd had to work up at the resort that day, but at least we'd been in the same city.

"By the way, Raven doesn't have to worry about that performance review anymore," said Mom.

"What do you mean?"

"I sent a letter to Snowbird and they changed her recommendation."

"What?"

"She can work there with no problem when she comes back. I made sure she had a review that took into account all her hard work."

"Didn't we specifically ask you not to get involved?"

"I just couldn't let anyone say bad things about Raven."

"Mom, you can't do things like that. We're adults."

"You're my children."

"We can handle things like this ourselves."

"I know you can."

I sighed.

As embarrassing as it is to have my mother call and write to people on my behalf whether I want her to or not, it is also endearing. She cannot help herself. It is her nature to defend her family, to protect my sister and I and now Raven from whatever threats she sees in the world.

My mother in law, Phyllis, is similarly exasperating. When she visits us in Salt Lake, she does not allow us to spend any money. Restaurants, movie theaters, clothes, groceries… She buys everything for us, even things we don't need or want. Her attitude towards her grandson is, if possible, even more neurotic. Since Raven has been pregnant, she's sent us a set of plates and silverware, a quilt, several toys, books, baby clothes in a number of different sizes, and all manner of other "necessities." She also drove from her home in Missouri down to Florida where my brother in law and his wife live and picked up their changing table, rocking chair, and high chair. She brought these items back to Missouri, washed them all thoroughly, and then drove them out to Utah for us.

When we bought a second hand crib, she was worried it wasn't safe enough for Ezra and offered to buy us a brand new one. Her concern for our welfare and that of her grandson is paramount. No power on earth could stop her from performing her sacred duties, the protection of her clan.

Both my mother and my mother in law are endowed with a kind of ferocity of which I have only the barest understanding. I have no doubt that I would die to protect my son. I would endure pain for him. I would spend any amount of money if I knew I could buy him lifelong safety and happiness, but I am nothing compared to my mothers. They are obsessed, possessed of an energy, a fury that renders them unreasonable and less than sane, and this affliction is not a temporary state. They exist like that, on a knife edge of instinct, ready to leap into action the moment one of their children is threatened.

This state of mind is at the heart of what it means to be a mother, and I am somewhat concerned at what may happen to my wife once our child is born. Will she, too, take utter leave of her rationality? Will I? And what if we don't? Does that make us bad parents? And will we be able to continue to fight as hard as we always have for each other? Will the love between the two of us be diminished somehow, or diverted, turned towards our child?

The irony of my mothers' attitudes and actions is that even with all their tenacity, with all of their love for us, their good intentions, there are threats that they ignore, even exacerbate somewhat in their fervor to take care of us. Their protection is limited. From teachers and sales associates, from bosses and the IRS, our mothers can shield us, but they can do nothing about far greater threats. Oil spills, toxic chemicals and climate change; in their fervor to protect us, they are contributing to these threats more than ever before.

It's hard to see my mothers' actions as anything but expressions of love. Surely that's what they are. They are gifts given from the heart, or from some deeper, more primal place than that. They are born of survival and love and sacrifice, and because of that it is difficult to refuse them, difficult to say no. These gifts and protections are more than we need, more than I can stand to accept, and yet I receive them with reverence because of what they represent.

I am trying to be smarter than my parents were when they were raising me. I want to teach my son that consumption is not equivalent to value, that the things he does for himself are worth more than the things I can do for him, and yet, I want Ezra not to roll his eyes when I speak, not to feel as though he has to rebel. I want to let him grow in whatever way seems fitting to him, but I don't know how. My culture holds me back.

It's learned behavior. More than that, it's instinct, powerful and unconscious. It's in my DNA to buy things, to focus on the most immediate and apparent threats, to make sure he is happy from day to day even at the expense of the rest of the species. Everyone else can suffer and die as long as he is safe and happy and taken care of. There is no way to outsmart my chemical components, the impulses that make me a parent.

This is the monster at the root of climate change. This is what makes consumption and safety and innovation and technology and greed and apathy and idiocy so impossible to resist. Climate change is just the tracks of the tiger, a mark in the dirt left by something dangerous and feral.

In having a son, I am inheriting an insane legacy. One that tells me being a good parent means not exposing my son to risk. One in which I cannot let an opportunity to shield him go by untaken. One in which his happiness depends on how much money I am able to spend on him, what schools he will go to, what material possessions he can call his own. It is not my mother telling me this. It is my own body.

This is a path of gentle destruction, the way we justify violence in the name of protection, of love.

In another context, these impulses are directly responsible for species survival. In places where there are real dangers like venomous animals and open wells, the instinct to protect becomes essential rather than misguided. Collecting and even hording resources allows a family or a village to survive in places where there are seasonal droughts or famines. These instincts are the difference between life and death.

From this perspective, it seems that it is not my mother who is insane, but rather that our world has become too gentle, too predictable for her wildest instincts.

Everything in American society reflects this gentleness, this ease of living. Every aspect of our society is built with an eye toward comfort or safety. Our food comes hygienically packaged with horns and hooves removed for our convenience. Our children are born in hospitals with teams of experts waiting in the wings in case something goes wrong. Our cars are built with seat belts and airbags to make sure that we won't ever die.

We are eased into our jobs with training programs and internships, eased into our homes with subsidized loans, eased into social relationships and dating through electronic media, eased into marriage, and eased back out again almost painlessly.

Our instincts betray us. In a gentle world, they are fierce and untamed. This is the irony, that our wildest instincts have led us towards civilization, imposed protection. We have made our bodies which are adapted to survival in the harshest conditions earth can offer, obsolete.

Perhaps climate change is an unconscious act of rebellion, a move towards chaos. Perhaps this is the only way our bodies can manage their equilibrium, by plunging us into uncertainty, into situations where we will, once again, have to fight for our lives. Maybe disaster is a natural consequence of too much stability. Maybe it is the way we resist control, the way we begin to fight back, to demand a world that demands much of us, one in which our survival instincts are again essential.

2.

You want to know how global climate destabilization looks? Look no further than your average third world country. On the one hand there are a hundred examples of the apocalypse during different decades in different parts of the world. People committing rape, murder, and genocide, countries with little or no infrastructure, but with stocks of AK-47s and anti aircraft rockets, countries in which people do battle for basic resources and human rights. The apocalyptic vision of the future presented in Cormac McCarthy's *The Road*, where resources have become scarce, and bands of beast-like men roam the countryside raping and pillaging the last vestiges of civilization, is or has been close to reality in places like Sudan, Rwanda, South Africa, Libya, Cambodia, Yugoslavia, Chechnya, Afghanistan… the list goes on.

The United States, too, has a history of genocide, systematic destruction of indigenous peoples and cultures and wars for resources. Our own Civil War was fought over human resources: slaves and the right to keep them. These kinds of scenarios are ones that will play out more frequently and in more secure parts of the world as climate change becomes more and more apparent. Decreases in the availability and increases in the price of fossil fuels are expected to cause food and water shortages across large swaths of the United States. As resources become scarce, many people predict that outbreaks of violence will become the norm. Thus far, most people are unwilling to speculate about which groups of people will likely take control of scant resources and which groups will be the victims in such a conflict. I suspect such delineation will occur along historic fault lines. Brown people verses white people, those who believe in a certain incarnation of God verses everyone else, those with money or power against those without.

The other possibility I see for how we, as a species, will deal with climate change is just as grave, but more optimistic. Other third world countries serve as the example for this milder adaptation. Kiribati, Nauru, Bhutan, and a handful of other nations have managed to thrive with scant resources and limited Western influence and technology. These countries boast small population centers, infrastructure built with mostly local materials and economies that function less on money and fossil fuels and more on locally available goods and services. Not everything about this model is good. Kiribati has a high infant mortality rate, and zero I-Kiribati doctors. The healthcare system, in general, is abysmal, and there are few opportunities for higher education. Most educated Westerners would call Kiribati living standards poor and their way of life backward. Despite this, given the choice between wholesale destruction or a peaceful society with slightly lower standards of living, I know which one I would choose.

But is that it? Will we be forced to choose between violence and poverty? Is there some other option I can't yet see? Rebecca Solnit alludes to such an alternative in *A Paradise Built in Hell* when she examines catastrophe and finds that it brings out the best in people rather than the worst. In times of crisis, she contends, people tend towards altruism, empathy, and kindness rather than cruelty or violence. For evidence, she cites the actions of the people of New York in the wake of the 9/11 tragedy. Many people risked their lives to help out fellow New Yorkers rushing into the cloud of toxic debris to rescue survivors.

Perhaps there are stores of untapped heroism waiting inside each of us like pine cones waiting for a forest fire to open them and release their seeds. I would like to think so, but I'm wary. This disaster is breaking over us now in a hundred small ways and so far it has failed to catalyze us into action.

Touch

The change has been too gentle. We are easing ourselves into disaster, getting used to it. What happens if there is no perceptible change in us, no sharp sudden shock, just the gradual downward spiral into madness and pain?

Destruction is simple. Close your eyes.

3.

We are on a beach on Plum Island off the east coast of Massachusetts, my mother and I, walking along the shoreline. It is summer vacation. We are staying in my uncle's beach house. We've spent the day shopping in Newburyport at the local tourist traps: Screen printed T-shirts, cheap sunglasses, knick knacks made from shells or beach glass. It's night now. The stars are the only light. We are talking, listening to the sounds of the waves, feeling the breeze, fresh and cold, as it rolls in from somewhere out over the dark water. We stop and stand, still in the pale light looking out over the sea, my mother's arm around my waist, mine around her shoulders, almost on top of her head because of the difference in our heights.

The walks we take are a vacation ritual. After the sun sets, we sit and wait for the temperature to drop and then put on windbreakers and sweatshirts and head to the water. Whoever wants to come is welcome, but tonight, my sister and father are too tired. They've gone to bed early and it's just us, the two of us, together as we were sixteen years ago for nine months before my birth. We stand, a lanky teenage boy and a short middle aged woman, each enjoying the other's company, more than that, the connection between us, of blood and bone. We are so similar, more like each other than any other living things on the island. Beyond our skin, we feel the darkness, the void of unfamiliar matter, but between us there is recognition, heat, a vital energy.

There is a bright flash, an arc burned across the sky, beautiful and silent stretching from one horizon to the other, and we bear witness to its cold, blue light.

Touch

It is as if this falling star were meant only for us, a sign in a language neither of us can read, but unmistakable.

We stand for a long time after that, looking out over the Atlantic, both unwilling to let the moment die. And then we each glance at the other, our arms fall to our sides, and we turn and walk up the beach toward the house.

I have thought of that star often, as often as I think of my mother. That moment is part of us, inseparable from the connection between our bodies. When I think of my mother, the light of that glowing arc illuminates her. It is the moment of awareness, the way we know one another through our own skin. The ways we are like each other, my face reflecting her dimples, my eyes the same shade of blue. The half of me is contained in her DNA. The way part of what it means to be a man comes from her, from the feminine. The way her body shapes me. The way mine shapes her. We have been infused with each other, with that beach, that starlight, that sand beneath us, that breeze swelling our hair, that one falling star. It is her arms around me so that even when we are apart, I feel her embrace, and that of every other living thing to which I bear witness.

Connection, too, is simple, and salvation, redemption, kindness: open your eyes!

KAIBOBOKI

Kaiboboki had three sons, beautiful boys with dark brown skin and sleek black hair. They couldn't have been more than two years apart from one another. The youngest was five or six, the oldest ten.

Most of the kids in the village floated around. They wandered in and out of people's compounds and they were fed and hugged and cared for by whoever happened to be around. It was hard to tell which children belonged to whom, but Kaiboboki's sons were easy to spot because they were so handsome and they never seemed to stray as far from home as the other children. Perhaps they had instructions to this effect, or perhaps they simply preferred their own home and their own parents.

Kaiboboki lived across the road from us. It was a dirt road and it didn't go very far, only a few hundred feet from the main gravel road to the middle school near our house. Hardly anyone ever drove down it. His house was like ours, made of sticks and twine. He had a buia, a raised platform with a thatched roof, in the yard like a deck. I hardly ever saw him on it, though. He was usually out doing something, fishing, repairing thatch, talking to people. He was very popular in the village.

When we arrived on Abaiang, Kaiboboki was one of the first teachers at the Junior Secondary School to approach me about helping him with his lessons. His English was terrible at the time, like my Kiribati, and though he was a math teacher, all his text books were written in English and his curriculum was supposed to be taught in English.

As for me, I was the new guy in the village, an unknown quantity, and white, which is to say, highly inept by reputation. It was a brave move on his part to come and talk to me.

We planned out his lessons together, and I taught with him for a while. Each of us would take one section of the lesson and explain it, and then we'd both walk around the room as the students tried to work out the math problems we'd copied out for them on the blackboard.

Later on, Kaiboboki also helped my wife and me start a preschool in the village and he asked us to help him coach a girls' soccer and volleyball team.

I liked him. He was a good neighbor, constantly going out of his way to make sure we felt comfortable and cared for, and he was bright. His English improved rapidly so that by the end of our two-year term, he was one of the best in the village. He was immensely helpful, too. When our pit toilet filled up, it was he who capped it with cement and helped us dig a new one. We reciprocated as best we could. When our banana tree put out a bunch, we made banana bread and took some over to his house.

He was sitting on his buia when we brought the bread over and he sat up straight when he saw it. His eyes seemed to grow wider and brighter and he accepted it with such reverence it was almost comical.

"It will be for the boys," he said. And he made us sit as he called his sons to him and divided the loaf among them. They ate it in silence sitting as proud and straight as their father. There was a feeling of piety that made us feel uncomfortable, and after a while we left awkwardly. To us it was only bread. To Kaiboboki, it had been something more. The significance of such acts, of giving and receiving was more profound than I was used to. It was an incongruity between our two cultures that we never reconciled, a misunderstanding, a gap in communication.

*   *   *

There is something else I have to tell, and I do it reluctantly. Kaiboboki was a good friend, a good person, a good father. That is how I remember him, but I remember darker things, too, that I never saw, but heard.

Sometimes in the evenings we would be sitting in our house, Raven and I, playing cards or reading and we'd hear it, crying from across the street. Not soft crying, not the kind that one does in private, head in the crook of an arm, but hysterical, horrid, frightened crying, a scream broken into sobs, and we'd hear the sharp thwack of wood on flesh a high pitched wail, and again the sick sound, and the voice wailing words into the still night, "Kabara au bure, kabara au bure!" "I'm sorry, I'm sorry!" Over and over, the words punctuated with blows. Sometimes it lasted for only a few minutes, and sometimes much longer. Sometimes there were two voices or three crying, and sometimes only one.

Each time this happened we would sit in silence, look at each other, horrified, or stare off into the shadowy corners of the room. Afterwards, Raven would sometimes cry and I would hold her in silence until she recovered and then we would resume our game, but with a feeling that something was broken, something that perhaps could not be fixed.

Kaiboboki's children were, by no means, the only children in the village who received beatings. Many of the schools on the island used corporal punishment as a means of discipline, though neither

Raven's school nor mine participated in such cruelty. But almost every parent in our village hit their children from time to time. It was an accepted part of culture. I knew it happened. We'd even been warned in our training that we would see things like this in our village. We were told that our reaction to it was up to us. We could say something about it and risk alienating our community, or we could put up with it as part of the culture.

In the end, we placed ourselves somewhere in between. I never approached Kaiboboki about it individually. I knew the statistics, that victims of abuse are more likely to abuse their own children. I knew that it was wrong, but I never did anything to try and make him stop.

We did address the issue at a meeting we held in our village for international women's day. Most of our friends and neighbors showed up including Kaiboboki and his wife, and we role played positive discipline techniques like praising good behavior and talking about negative behavior rather than hitting. We felt good about it for a

Touch

while, like we'd done something, but the beatings continued. We heard them and it was proof to us of failure.

I'm not sure that my saying something directly to Kaiboboki would've stopped it. He might have listened to me and continued to hit his kids. He might have stopped while I was living across from him and continued as soon as I left. He may have denied ever doing it in the first place. Too, it is a hard thing to change culture, and however onerous, however evil, this was culture. Who was I to step in and denounce it? Sure, child abuse is wrong, that part is easy, but once you start changing things, where does it end? Is it child abuse to allow kids to contract and die from easily preventable diseases? Do you insist on Western medicine? Do you put in a water treatment plant? That requires electricity to run, so do you put in a diesel generator? There is no source of diesel, so should you advocate importing it? You need money to import fuel, so do you open the reef to divers on holiday from England, France, and the United

States? This means a new airport, a hotel, or a chain of hotels, restaurants, taxi service, and gift shops. New abuses in the name of eradicating old ones.

You cannot change only one thing. You have to choose. For right or wrong, I chose Kiribati, and I think I would choose it still.

I've never given much thought to whether or not my neighbors beat their children before or since. There are walls in the place I live now, thick walls that block out most of the sound. When I do hear anything from the neighbors, a radio or television turned up too loud, I pretend not to.

*   *   *

When I was young, my family had a wood stove. We had central air too, and a furnace, but the stove was what we used to heat the house. The furnace was backup. My dad would cut stove lengths in the winter and I would chop the wood into usable pieces with a maul. The head of it was a solid triangular piece of steel and the shaft was a hollow steel pipe three feet long. It must've

Touch

weighed twenty pounds. I would lift it high and then let the end fall onto the logs. Sometimes it went through the wood as easily as water. Other times, the blade would turn and the flat of the head would strike frozen wood. The resulting vibrations would ring my bones.

When the wood was chopped, my father and I hauled it down to the front of the house and stacked it. Sometimes the pile would go all the way to the eaves of the house. It was hard work to keep the woodbox full, but it was also satisfying to chop for a few hours and see the steam begin to unfurl from my body. We were men, and this was what it meant to be so.

It was satisfying, too, to know that our heat came out of our labor, mine and my father's, and my mother's too. She would set the fire in the stove, would add the wood when it burned low to rekindle it. We were keepers of the flame. This was our culture.

The thermostat for the furnace was in the same room as the stove, and it was a mark of pride that the furnace would not kick on as long as the fire was going strong. All of our bedrooms, mine, my parents', my sister's were in other parts of the house, and when I finally went to bed, it would take ten or fifteen minutes of shivering and rubbing my limbs together to get comfortable under the blankets, but we put up with it, enjoyed it even because of the fire.

Later, my parents moved to a house with a gas stove instead of a wood-burning one, and I moved to an apartment. Even if I had a stove or a fireplace, living in Salt Lake City means that I would have to buy wood rather than cut it.

I still sit in my apartment huddled under my blankets at night, trying not to turn on my heater until it is absolutely necessary. It is a holdover from a former life.

At some point the cold is too much and I flip the switch and feel the warm air on my skin as the heat kicks on. I think of chopping wood, the lift and release of the maul, the drawn out rending sound of a log reluctantly coming apart. I feel the cold air in my nostrils, the sweat on my brow, the muscle memory of drawing back and striking. This is in me. It's not abuse. There's no flesh involved, but there's a connection. The physicality of these acts imbues them with significance. It is a way to work things out, and perhaps that is at the roots of what it means to be a man, to be human. I connect through action, through my skin. There's no other way. So much is lost in the flip of a switch, the turning of a dial.

*   *   *

When we left our island for the last time, we gave out gifts. I gave Kaiboboki a suitcase, some shirts, and a new knife. He thanked me, and I stood there, both of us stood there, waiting for something. I wanted him to understand that he was my friend, to let him know how much that meant to me.

For me, the appropriate thing would have been a hug, but in Kiribati, men don't do this, so we looked at each other and finally shook hands. His were rough and strong, calloused from fishing and tying thatch. Mine were soft with easy living. I remember thinking how kind those hands had been, how much they had done for us, and yet there was a brutality there as well, a terrible kind of violence.

I'm trying hard to understand this, to believe that my friend did not mean what he did. That he simply knew no other way. It's a lie. This was part of who he was. Perhaps he could have changed, but these things were there within him, were part of the legacy he was passing on to his sons. Sometimes I think it's right that Kiribati should go underwater. It would be fitting, just. It would simplify matters. I wouldn't have to feel as I do about the place. It's been three years now since I lived there, and it haunts me, knowing that there is a whole country full Kaibobokis, that each one of them must choose to hit his kids or not, and that even though I was there, even though the answer was absolute, even though it is wrong to hit your sons no matter what, I could do nothing about it. When Abaiang goes underwater, perhaps my guilt and frustration will go with it.

Touch

And then I think of his sons, my own, unborn son, and I understand that I cannot drown my guilt, nor sink it because the abuse I am responsible for is not so much symbolized in the land, but in the rising tide. Even when Abaiang slides beneath the waves, the tides will still be there. They will rise and recede and at their lowest, the reef, the bones of the island, will be revealed, a reminder of destruction. I think of Kaiboboki, my friend, reverently breaking bread for his sons. Things can change. They have to.

We let go each other's hands and smiled at one another, and Kaiboboki placed a garland of flowers on my head to honor me. His sons stood behind him straight backed and proud, boys trying hard to be men.

I DON'T GIVE A DAMN ABOUT CLIMATE CHANGE!

Suddenly in perfect detail, I pictured the burrowing owls' mound—that clay–covered fist rising from the alkaline flats. The exact one these beergut-over-beltbuckled men had leveled.

I walked calmly over to their truck and leaned my stomach against their door. I held up my fist a few inches from the driver's face and slowly lifted my middle finger to the sky.

This is for you—from the owls and me.

– Terry Tempest Williams (from *Refuge*)

Missouri, 2007

When we left Kiribati, we made a few mistakes. The Peace Corps warned us that probably no one would care about our experiences the way we wanted them to. People have a hard time visualizing places they've never been to. To the uninitiated, our country could never be real. The literature we received prior to coming home recommended that we stay calm and adjust slowly to life back in America. In time, they said, your service will fall into perspective, and it will be easier to talk about. We didn't listen. The morning we got back to the states, we began to talk passionately about life in our village to anyone who would sit still long enough.

We babbled about how much we were going to miss our dog and two cats, whom we'd left behind, about the fact that our friend Kimeata was going to be moving into our old house, about how we'd heard that Jackie Chan was dead. He wasn't, but the fact seemed a relief to us rather than the anticlimax it was for our friends. I'm not even sure where we heard such a rumor, but Raven and I had spent days shaking our heads, believing the kung fu master had passed away from a sudden heart attack.

None of our conversations were based on shared experience. They were one sided, misguided soliloquies that made only the remotest sense to our friends and loved ones. It's not that They weren't interested in our service, but to us, it seemed like they wanted to know only in the most superficial aspects of our time there.

We got the same questions over and over. Did you like it there? What did you do there?

What do they eat? My god, how to answer any of those? If you have lived in a foreign country for any amount of time, you know that it is complicated. Some days it was miserable and other days it was paradise, but each day was different, full of unique and beautiful experiences that could not be contained by any sort of generalization. How could we sum up our experiences in a few words? The glib answers that were expected of us, and that we grudgingly gave, were enough to satisfy our audiences, but not for us. Our words were unable to convey the things we wanted to say about the place. Instead, they seemed to diminish our rich memories, and we pined for the loss.

Peace Corps tried to warn us about culture shock, too. They said we would go through a period of depression and anxiety as we tried to readjust to life in America.

The same day we landed in St. Louis, we visited the store. We needed toiletries: shampoo, toothbrushes, deodorant, all the accoutrement of modern life that we had so carelessly dispensed

Touch

with on Abaiang. Wal-Mart was the place to go. We parked and walked across the blacktop toward the automatic doors. I remember feeling excited to see what was inside, to revel in the glory of such a huge, full place, one that had everything my heart could desire. But as we drew near the air conditioned monstrosity, I also began feeling uncomfortable. There were so many people here, big fat people in camouflage. I didn't know any of them.

My heart was pounding as we entered and all at once, I felt as though I could not get enough air. I concentrated on my breathing, pushed the panic down. There were so many things and all in the open where I could touch them and put them into my basket, could take what I liked and bring it home with me. Instead of exhilarated, I felt overwhelmed.

We walked slowly and picked, one by one, the items on our list. We put them into the basket and walked it toward the front of the store. We slid our credit card, took our bags, all the while with a shared feeling of discomfort at the ease of it, at the strange transaction that involved no words. The silence seemed to tower over us.

It was like that all the time, everywhere we went. There were sounds alright, the noise of traffic, the din of the radio and television, people's voices even, sounds so loud they hurt our ears, but a silence too, an absence, of waves perhaps or the wind in the branches, the voices of friends and loved ones we'd left behind, of a different kind of silence, one more profound and beautiful that would not come to us here though we searched for it.

The anxiety I felt in Wal-Mart was not the first hint of my peculiar disease, but it was the most acute of a lifetime's worth of anxiety that seems always to have existed for me in the retail spaces of the world. When I am forced to go to a store, I get flustered and uncomfortable. It's happened to me for years and I can't seem to trace its origins. Perhaps it goes back to a time when I bought something with hard earned money and was disappointed, a toy of some sort that broke the first time I used it. I don't know. What I do know is that it occurs whenever there is the possibility of a certain type of transaction.

It makes me feel dirty to exchange money for goods. That is the simplest way I can put it. It is an unequal transaction, or at least unknown, the way money changes value, the way it is paper, insubstantial in the hand, so easy to give and receive. It makes me uncomfortable. There's something about the expectation of receiving something, and because the acquisition is effortless, the thing itself loses value. I've always felt a vague gnawing guilt about buying things, but it took coming home from Kiribati to awaken me to exactly what it meant. I had always been missing something without realizing it. I still didn't know exactly what was missing, but now I could at least see the shape of the hole.

Sonoran Desert, 2002

It's night in the desert west of Prescott, AZ, and the stars shine fierce and bright through the cold air. I am tucked into my sleeping bag without a pad or a tent or a pillow. I toss and turn and cinch the draw cords tight around my face. I sleep fitfully. It's so cold. My breath fogs in the air, condenses on the blue nylon. I doze, and wake, shivering. At one point my legs are on top of her sleeping bag. Courtney does not stir, but sleeps soundly as though she's part of the wash, a piece of sandstone, carved from the desert. I curl my body around hers, aware of how close we are, of her skin beneath the fabric of her bag. She sleeps on and I doze again and wake in the pale light of dawn with my face in the dust.

A low rise of desert scrub casts its shadow over us, and I look down from our shelf of hard, cold ground into an orchard and a marsh beyond. The land is called Bingham Cienega. It is a wetland in the desert, a place where a spring bubbles ancient water just below the surface of the land. There are tall grasses and trees here, cottonwoods and willows, and, of course, apple trees on the near side of the lowland, the ranch's orchard. Bingham

Ranch is a sustainable ranch. The new owners have chosen to limit their herds and restore some of the previously overgrazed landscape to its former glory.

We're here to help. We're planting willows in the marsh as erosion control and a windbreak for the orchard. After breakfast, we receive our instructions. Willows grow from cuttings and the owners have cut poles from grown trees, hundreds of them. We are to walk through the marsh planting poles. This proves to be much easier said than done. The poles are four feet long, straight and gray. I take ten at a time under my arm and walk out into the marsh. It is muddy, as marshes tend to be, and in no time I'm slogging through dense grass in water and Earth up to my knees. Every thirty or so steps, I pull one of the poles from my awkward bundle, grasp it by one end and force it as deep as I can into the mud with a soft squelch. It is oddly satisfying, like impaling some soft bodied beast. By lunch time, I'm soaked and dirty and I've barely covered a mile.

The ground behind me looks like a half-destroyed comb, tines poking out of it at irregular intervals. I move towards her confidently, my steps slow, but sure. I have learned this landscape, learned to turn my foot just so to release it from the mud, to hold onto one of the willow poles for balance. Courtney makes her way toward me, and she moves as comfortably as I move. She, too, has learned the landscape, and for a moment, I convince myself that it is her I am in love with.

Courtney is new, it's her first trip. We are dating. Ultimately, it will not go anywhere, and that's okay, though at the moment she seems like a very important person in my life.

She comes with me often at first, out into the desert to build trail, or hike, or simply to be with the land, to lie down on it and feel the weight of an immense sky, but as time goes on, the relationship fades. She spends less and less time outdoors, and I realize that it was never her, only willows and Earth. She was a sojourner, a visitor and now she is gone. The loss is almost nothing.

Touch

I am forging my life from this, from muscle memory, from repetition, the driving action of forcing pole into marsh. This is what becomes important, water and wood grains and the knowledge that these branches will become willows, the act of planting, and of walking through mud, and hardpan, the sting of dry air in my lungs, the smell of dust.

Appalachian Trail, 2008

Raven and I began hiking the Appalachian Trail in February of 2008 as a reintroduction to America, a renewal of spirit. We'd returned from the Peace Corps in October, and had been appalled to find excess everywhere we looked. In the store, there were thirty kinds of toothpaste, and each of them came in a box which served no other purpose but to be thrown away as soon as it was opened. Every meal we sat down to seemed three or four times bigger than we could possibly eat. Driving on the highway seemed way too fast.

In addition to all the waste, there were things missing. Colors seemed less vibrant. In Kiribati, green had meant a thousand different shades all pressed together in the dense foliage of the jungle. Blue had been waves of deep sapphire, the turquoise sea, the velvety richness of almost dusk. The pungent smell of the lagoon was gone, too, replaced by the sickening undertones of petrochemicals, diesel exhaust, and espresso. America seemed dead.

The AT was an antidote, we thought, a way to find some other part of America, one still alive, still rooted in the hard Earth, so we began in February. I'd managed to convince Raven that Georgia, the southern terminus of the trail, was so far south it would be balmy, even in winter. By the time we reached Virginia, she still had not forgiven me. It turns out that Georgia does, in fact, get very cold, even to the point of snow and ice storms like the one that was in full swing the morning we started hiking. Now, at the end of April, as the spring finally began to peak, I had high hopes that all that misery was behind us.

We were nearing Pearisburg, Virginia, and the dense tree cover had broken for a moment as we walked near a wide bike path. The sun broke through the foliage, and for the first time in days I felt warm. We paused to bask in the light momentarily and then walked on. The trail joined, presently, with the bike path and the walking became easier. It was flat and paved, unlike the rocky ruts we'd been treading up and down the side of every mountain from here to Georgia.

Presently we came to a bridge, and looking down from it, we realized the stream we were crossing was a familiar one. It had been photographed recently for a news story. Someone had shot two fishermen here about a month ago. Neither of them had died, but the same shooter had murdered two women near here in 1981. He'd been released from prison only a few days before. The man had crashed the fishermen's truck into a tree that same evening and died of his injuries.

"They weren't hikers though," I said.

"No, they weren't," said Raven. That calmed us somehow. "Still, it's scary to think about."

"They were just in the wrong place at the wrong time." Raven looked down as she hiked. I could tell the conversation was upsetting her.

"Don't worry, baby, the chances of getting shot on the Appalachian Trail are still really miniscule. There's something like five thousand people who hike every year and those guys are the only ones who got shot. We're safer than if we were driving."

"I'm glad we took that break in Damascus." We'd stopped an extra day there. I was sure that wasn't the difference between life and death, but I nodded anyway. "I'm glad we're slow hikers," she said. We both laughed.

This was familiar territory for us: close calls, unsafe conditions, dangerous living. These things had been commonplace for the first two years of our marriage. Raven and I had gotten married a mere six months before leaving for Abaiang.

Abaiang, where there was no qualified doctor. Abaiang, where we drew our drinking water from an uncovered well. Abaiang, where the emergency tsunami plan included strapping on our bike helmets and life jackets and climbing a coconut tree. We were familiar with uncertainty, but there was a difference. The murder rate on Abaiang was zero and had been for over ten years. Plus, there was nowhere to go. The whole island was only twenty miles long and less than a half mile wide. There were only a handful of trucks and a few motorbikes. The dangers were all of a different sort. They were still, patient dangers, disease and madness.

On the other hand, this year was about movement. It was the step, sure and strong, the feel of rock under the boot, the gentle sway of pack on shoulders, how the hip strap raises and settles the load on the bones. It was the necessary working of physical things through the body.

One morning we woke up to find that freezing rain had fallen in the night and cemented into a hard crust over the fabric of our tent so that we could not work the zippers. We lay there for hours waiting for sunlight to pierce the thick fog and melt us out. Eventually, we had to shake the tent from within like a shiver, casting bits of icy exoskeleton onto the frozen ground. What must it have looked like from the outside, some blue green glistening behemoth shaking itself to life and then opening to reveal us two like hatchlings, or the serpent ends of new sown seeds.

We were reborn through movement. Each step we took was towards some end, and the end was well defined: Katahdin. A mountain in Maine, tangible and accessible if distant. Abaiang was all waiting, for boats and planes, for things to begin, for people to show up, for the seas to rise and wash us away. Here, we rushed forward, hungry for milemarkers, checkpoints. A way to measure ourselves, our movement.

We didn't spend too long in any one place. We feared idleness, inaction. Every interaction we had, every exchange cloyed. Movement corroborated the illusion that we could escape. So we moved on through the Smokies, the Shenandoahs, the Hogbacks.

But as we moved steadily northward, we began to hike more and more slowly. My joints swelled. Raven's knees and back began to ache all the time.

In New Jersey, we finally broke down completely. We spent three nights in the worst hotel I can imagine. Simply uttering the name, The Doyle, makes me shudder. There was black mold in the shower and the mattress was stained with blood. I found a bull's-eye shaped rash under Raven's arm. Lyme Disease. And I developed a terrible fever. Katahdin remained hidden beyond the horizon. Our bodies had reached their limits. We tried to go on, but in Pawling, New York were forced to abandon the attempt eight hundred miles short of the end.

Salt Lake City, 2010

I've spent the day watching coverage of the Deep Water Horizon blowout. They've fixed a cap over the pipe and the flow of oil into the Gulf has finally slowed.

We are in our bed, emotionally exhausted by the prospect of so much despair. We lay naked together, Raven and I, touch skin on skin and I put my head on her belly to get close to our unborn baby. What a world we are bringing you into, I think.

You are not allowed to touch certain places in the Gulf anymore. They are toxic with crude oil and corexit. If you ran your fingers through the sand, the chemicals would enter your skin and you would feel the disease. It's not safe, this world, this ocean, this life, and yet I long to have the water run through my fingers, silky and smooth, to have the sand give softly under my feet, to feel the brush of seaweed, the feathers of gull wings.

Touch

There is a hormone called Oxytocin that is released by the brain when we experience skin to skin contact. More of it is released from contact with more sensitive skin. The hands are good, the neck is better, the lips cause it to gush forth. That's why kissing feels so good. It is a contact high.

Oxytocin is also present during orgasm, both male and female, and is important in the birthing process because it stimulates labor. Recent research shows that the presence of Oxytocin is one of the prime factors in healthy interpersonal relationships. Memories of positive relationships cause increases of the hormone in some women, and it appears to be important to the process of mother and infant bonding ("I Get a Kick").

It is an addiction between people, a chemical dependence on physical interaction, on love in its rawest form.

Is it any wonder I fell in love with the desert, with Kiribati, with the AT, with my wife? Is it any wonder I've fallen in love with my unborn child? These relationships are founded on contact, on touch, and intimacy. I cannot help but love gray barked willows, sand, the skin over my wife's heart. These things are like my own body now. I've taken them into me with all their salts, and poisons, all of their softnesses and vulnerabilities. The Gulf is there too, though I haven't been back in years, but I remember the velvety warm waves, the soft grittiness of live sand dollars, the pebbly skin of starfish.

I am poisoned. That's the truth of it. It is a cancer, epidemic, ubiquitous. It is the world inside me, growing with unlimited potential, with no restraint. It is our response to poison. Grow. Grow. Grow. Grow until you die. Grow until the very heart of you, the DNA, the marrow of your bones becomes a poison in its own right.

All of it is inside of me. Kiribati, the Appalachian Trail, the Sonoran desert, failure, poison, guilt. All of it.

That's the point. I have tried and failed to live only the beautiful bits of life, the satisfying parts made of pure things like water and sand and love. I have fallen off the map a number of times looking for meaning, or at least a way to live consistently. There is no such way.

Kiribati, 2006

The wa[10] ride from Abaiang to Tarawa is one of the most hellish experiences of my life. The wa is not a large affair. It is wooden, painted bright yellow and red, large enough to hold fifty or so people comfortably. There are at least a hundred of us sitting on woven mats on the deck of the boat, or standing and holding onto the beams of the sun shade. Some of us are already sprawled out on top of each other trying to sleep. We've taken the wa because we're transporting our dog so she can have her only visit to the vet, who is actually not a vet. He is simply a man who has been trained to spay and neuter animals. We'd heard somewhere that the local airline doesn't transport animals. There's no official policy, no website or brochure in which to check this fact so we've taken the boat instead.

---

[10] Kiribati word for boat.

Twenty minutes into the voyage, which takes approximately eleven hours to complete, the dog, Snack, gets seasick. We move up to the fore of the boat which is not shaded and, therefore, has no people on it. Snack is sick five more times before we reach Tarawa. We feel bad for her. She's so uncomfortable. We're not particularly comfortable ourselves. We've covered ourselves in strips of fabric to protect us from the sun, but it's hot on the bow of the boat and we've only brought a liter of water a piece. We've packed small amounts of food to, but the beating sun and the smell of dog sick make us loath to eat anything. At one point a pod of dolphins breaks the surface of the water, pacing the boat for nearly half an hour like a consolation miracle. It's dusk before we arrive in Betio, the largest village on Tarawa, and we are exhausted and hungry. We take a bus, a minivan with ground effects lights and huge speakers that pump the bass from island music into my bones. We ride almost the length of the island, another hour because of the stops and starts the bus makes, back to the Peace

Corps dormitories in Bikenibeu. When we arrive, we tie the dog up outside with a dish of water and stumble wearily into the Chinese restaurant next door.

This place is a far cry from Abaiang where there are no restaurants and no busses. Our village on Abaiang is surrounded in either direction by at least a half mile of bush before a person reaches the next village. There is one working phone on the island, no running water, no electricity except from personal generators and a few solar panels.

On Tarawa, there are taps, cell phones, a central diesel generator. There is an unbroken line of homes, some constructed of concrete, that stretches the length of the island. There is air conditioning and an international airport, and two stores that carry alcohol. There are even two movie theaters. It is the pinnacle of civilization.

From another angle, Tarawa is a tiny place, which lacks infrastructure. It's home to less than fifty thousand people, smaller than most medium-sized cities in America. The island has a history of

Western (and Eastern) influence. During World War II, Tarawa was occupied by the Japanese who installed three Vickers antiship guns and a network of bunkers and machine gun nests. Because of its strategically located airfield, Betio became the scene of the bloodiest battle in Marine Corps history as troops stormed Red Beach at the end of the island. The guns and bunkers are still visible today and every so often visitors come across the bones of Japanese and American soldiers still half-buried in the sandy soil.

Today, Kiribati accepts aid from a variety of countries including Japan, the U.S., Australia, and, most importantly, Taiwan. Most of the aid comes in the form of infrastructure projects like roads and buildings, and most of the projects are here, on Tarawa. Because the island is not large, only about fifteen miles long and less than a half mile wide in most places, there is a problem with overcrowding. There is not much groundwater, little capacity for sewage, few places to build a new house. The lagoon, which once provided much of the food for

the island is polluted with petroleum runoff,
garbage, and human waste. It is one of the most
densely populated areas on the planet.

I am reminded of a passage from Annie
Dillard. "My point about rock barnacles is those
million million larvae 'in milky clouds' and those
shed flecks of skin. Sea water seems suddenly to be
but a broth of barnacle bits. Can I fancy that a
million million human infants are more real? What
if God has the same affectionate disregard for us
that we have for barnacles?" (166-167).

And yet we are relieved to be here, to order
spring rolls and lemon chicken off of the menu and
wait while it is prepared. We sleep, that night, in an
air conditioned room, take a hot shower, make tea
on the propane stove.

Tarawa, 2006

I helped the vet spay the dog. I held her legs
still as he cut into her and reached his fingers inside

to search for the fallopian tubes. This was the kindest thing for her, to rid her of the ability to have pups. There were already so many dogs roaming Abaiang in packs or kept in compounds as pets. There were so many and most were mangy and diseased, the kind of dogs that growl and sometimes bite, fearless and unhealthy. We threw rocks at them and hit them with sticks to keep them away. I often thought a dog hunting season would be a good solution to the overpopulation problem. We could reduce the size of the most vicious packs and feed people with fresh meat. It was win-win. .. as long as no one touched my dog. We loved Snack. She guarded us, slept under our buia at night, barked at intruders. She was our companion and friend in a place that could sometimes be very lonely. Not my dog. Nobody eats my dog.

Salt Lake City, 2006

I used to work at Planned Parenthood on a drug study. The drug was an alternative to plan B, the morning after pill. Women who had had unprotected sex could enter the study and earn 100 dollars for their time as well as a free dose of the drug, which was in its final stage of testing and had been shown to be very effective already. It was a good deal.

My job was to record answers to demographic questions, take a blood sample, and then give out the pill. The first part was difficult. I'd start with name and address and then transition into questions about the participants' sex lives. How many times in the past week? How recently? Have you taken emergency contraception before? How many times? These are the intimate questions a person wishes to share with no one. They trigger awkward and flustered responses, glances towards the door. After that, it was a relief to take blood, a bonding activity involving a certain amount of trust in the person with the needle, and a fulfillment of a commitment. I will not harm you.

We would return to my small office with the blood and I would rummage around for the pill and the cash which had become almost secondary to the transaction. Every participant received the pill with a sense of relief. They took it in their hands and put it quickly, reverentially into their mouths, swallowed, went out the door.

Living in Salt Lake City, I see a lot of mothers and fathers with what, to me, seems to be an enormous number of children. To be clear, I think four is an enormous number, but sometimes I see families of seven or eight people unloading themselves from a Ford Expedition. I'm appalled by it, by the crush of flesh, the sheer weight of all those children in one family. What immense amounts of food and toilet paper they must go through. How strange it is to imagine being part of such a family. I, myself, am one of only two children. When I see huge families, I always comment quietly to my wife. "Stop having kids," I say, or "They should've used birth control." Raven is much less judgmental. She tells me I can't say that about children already in existence. "You can't tell people they shouldn't have had their children." Her point is that parents always love their children.

Touch

They can't imagine their lives without each of their offspring because each one is special, unique, worthy of love. So there is a paradox. You can exhort people not to get pregnant, but once they've had babies, you'd better shut up.

We have a bias towards the particular, or against the general, the mass of heaving bodies that occupies Tarawa, the ones we don't know. There is a kind of relief in the idea. It's the reason for the nervousness in the women in my study, the reason they swallowed down the pill and left and forgot or tried to forget what happened. We are comfortable as long as they remain anonymous.

Once, the pill failed. All forms of birth control fail sometimes, and the effectiveness of emergency contraception tends to diminish the longer a person waits to take it. Perhaps this was the case. I don't know. I wasn't in charge of this particular patient, but I saw her as they walked her to a private room. Tears were streaming from her eyes because she was pregnant and what to do had suddenly become so much more complicated.

Tarawa is like that. You arrive believing there is a solution to this madness, to the heat and sweat and stench of low tide, to the overcrowding and pollution, and then you go into it and it becomes distinct. Meere and Tirenga and Rubenang. You hear their names and touch them, have meal together and the solutions melt away because there is no way to solve people you've come to love, no glib answers, and when people talk about climate change having a huge impact on the third world, you think, not my country, not Tarawa, not Kiribati.

Salt Lake City, 2010

Last week, the village of Tebunginako on Abaiang was washed away by the tides. Where the village used to be is a barren stretch of beach. Salt water has inundated the taro[11] pits. The coconut trees have all turned brown. The wells are filled with brine. The village is no longer livable.

---

[11] A large starchy root like casava.

Touch

Utah's official stance on climate change is that it does not exist. Presumably, there is a vast liberal conspiracy propagating the rumor that the Earth is warming due to carbon emissions.

So the Utah legislature is filled with idiots. It doesn't matter. With or without Utah's commiseration, Tebunginako is gone, wiped off the face of the Earth. *The Guardian* ran the story complete with pictures of people I knew. Kids Raven and I taught posed for the cameras ankle deep in salt water where their village used to be (McManus).

This is what we've lost, and we stand to lose so much more. I want to find the senators and representatives who voted for the resolution that stipulates the nonexistence of climate change in Utah. I want to find the authors of the Utah energy policy that recommends coal as a viable source of power for the foreseeable future. I want to find the authors of all such statements all across the United States, the owners of coal mines and energy companies, the lobbyists cutting down environmental legislation, every politician who takes money from big oil and coal. I want to find every son of a bitch who shrugs at the thought of climate change, every radio talk show host spouting poison and lies, every idiot telling us not to worry about it because it's a hoax or because scientists will find some way to fix it. I want to find them, and I want to burn their homes to the ground.

Abaiang, 2006

Let me begin again. We went fishing in the lagoon, Raven and I, in a red wa with a dozen men all carrying spear guns and knives. It was my friend Ian Toma's boat. We watched as the men donned snorkel masks and slid into the water trailing pandanus[12] logs tied to them with twine. We followed them in and watched from the surface as the men dived twenty feet down to the bottom of the lagoon.

The water was green and crystal clear and we could see them load the spear into the groove

---

[12] A type of fruit bearing tree used heavily in Kiribati for constructing homes and boats.

between thumb and forefinger and pull back the elastic bands as they neared a rocky outcropping, all dark caverns and coral.

One man reached a metal hook into a hole and pulled out an octopus. He rose with it, tentacles thrown backwards like long hair in a high wind, and dropped it over the side of the boat. Then he dived again. At another hole three men waited, spears drawn as a fourth hooked out a moray eel. They fired, one by one, sinking the steel shafts through its head. Still it struggled, writhing and fighting on the hook. That, too, went into the boat and flopped and twisted for ten minutes before it lay still.

Still other men picked up clamshells from the sea floor and split them with their knives. They dropped the meat into a bucket of brine to preserve it. We watched for an hour as the men harvested creatures from the lagoon and then we climbed into the boat. We needed a rest and Ian Toma started the engine and took us to a nearby island where he found us green coconuts and husked them for us.

We stayed there for two more hours while the men dove over and over again in the lagoon tying what they caught to their wooden floats. When we returned, the men climbed in and we returned to the village. We were exhausted, but the men were happy, boisterous. The bottom of the boat was filled with octopi and eels and fish they'd shot. The bucket of brine was full of clams. The men ate the extras that wouldn't fit raw, and rinsed themselves with the juice of green coconuts we'd gathered for them.

This is what I saw. This is what I experienced. For what it's worth, these things still exist.

Salt Lake City, 2010

My son is now lime sized. Raven cannot yet feel him. I cannot yet hear his heartbeat unaided, though I try. I put my ear to my wife's belly and listen. I hear the chemical gurgles of her intestines. I feel the warmth of her skin just below her navel. No baby. It does not worry me. I am not supposed to be able to hear him. He is not big enough yet. Next month, Raven will begin to feel him kick and he will double in size until he weighs more than a pound. It is strange, this reverse death, the furtive stirrings of becoming. Cell by cell, this child builds himself inside of my wife, a little at a time. One day, he begins to hear. Another, to swallow, a third, to sense light. It is a gradual awakening, a coming into consciousness.

I read somewhere that babies do not differentiate between themselves and the rest of the world for some time. Instead, everything they see and hear and feel, they integrate as a part of themselves. When they do begin to differentiate, to see themselves as other, it is traumatic. Life becomes a series of separations. First, my child will discover that he has no control over the rest of the world. Then, he will discover that we are separate, he and his mother and I, and he will feel all alone. If he is lucky, he will grow up and find that the world is broken, that there is death and misery, and that he cannot escape from that, cannot avoid or lessen the suffering.

This is the ritual, the legacy, the thing that is passed between us. There is no way to save the world. All there is is to be in it, to feel it, to suck out the poison through our own bodies, to try and share the weight of it.

THE CAUTIONARY TALE OF
TIM DECHRISTOPHER

I am outside of a courtroom in the Salt Lake City federal courthouse waiting to hear whether my friend will be found guilty of a crime he committed. Tim is inside the courtroom with his lawyers, while the rest of us, the prosecution, the judge and bailiff, and all the observers of the trial have left. The jury is out, has been for two hours now. I am pacing or looking in the windows of the courtroom or making awkward conversation with Tim's mother and sister who have both travelled from Colorado to attend the trial. I've offered my condolences on the fact that Tim is facing trial at all, tried to sound upbeat and hopeful about the outcome, attempted to offer restaurant suggestions for their stay. I am trying not to talk about the trial itself, which has been little more than a show trial, a way for the BLM and the district attorney to say that they gave Tim his day in court. Tim's sister and mother don't even seem to be listening to me. They look stressed and anxious. They know what's coming. We all do.

I have known Tim for more than a decade. We met when we were both students at Arizona State University, and we struck up a friendship based on our mutual desire to be outside, in the desert as much as possible. We hiked together, camped together, built trail together. Tim was even one of the groomsmen at my wedding. We've known each other about as well as two people can at times. After Tim dropped out of college, we went our own ways, but have always kept in touch, and now he is in a serious situation. I'm here. Where else would I be?

Outside the courtroom, the trial has been widely reported and it looks very much like an environmental case. Tim stepped in and disrupted an oil and gas lease auction in December of 2008. He had arrived at the auction after taking an economics final intending to join a protest in progress outside the building, but he went inside instead, registered as a bidder and won the rights to explore for oil and gas on several parcels of land.

Tim has given interview after interview to the press and each one is about the same thing: climate change. His motivations for his action are based on his belief that burning fossil fuels will eventually make Earth unlivable. He stepped in and bid on those parcels of land to keep them out of the hands of oil companies, to keep oil in the ground.

In the courtroom, the story has been quite different. The judge assigned to the trial, Dee Benson, who, incidentally, used to be Orrin Hatch's chief of staff, has set strict limits on the kind of testimony that is allowed to be presented to the jury. In three days there has been no mention of climate change, no talk of environmental motives, no suggestion of motive at all.

The argument has come down to a signature on a piece of paper and what it means. The question is whether Tim intended, when he signed the BLM contract to become a bidder, to pay for any bids he won. Testimony as to Tim's intelligence, whether he was smart enough to understand the contract, as to his intent, whether his actions were premeditated, and whether he understood the bidding process are all considered relevant, but nothing about why he did what he did.

I have to leave before the jury comes back. I have to go to work. It's raining outside as I board the eastbound train out of the city. No verdict yet. I send the message to my mom and dad and all my friends who have not been able to attend the trial.

*   *   *

This trial has caused me to think closely about my own responsibilities as an activist. When I first heard about Tim's actions, three days after the fact, I was shocked, but proud. Here was a man, a friend of mine standing up against a corrupt and short sighted government agency. I called him the morning I found out about it to tell him that I was with him, that he could count on me. In the back of my mind I wondered why I had not thought to do something similar. We were both environmentalists after all. Why wasn't I getting in the way of oil company land grabs.

Touch

He told me the story of how he'd gone into the room with the thought of making a speech to the oilmen and how it had occurred to him that he could make a much bigger difference by bidding on the land than by causing a disruption. I was exhilarated by his story. I thought of a hundred ways I could make a stand, too.

I could stand in the way of a coal truck, or tie myself to a tree in a forest marked for clear cutting. I could handcuff myself to a drilling rig somewhere in the oilfields of Colorado.

When I finally put down the phone, my mind was reeling. I sat down with Raven and we had breakfast in near silence. We were both astounded. Over the next few days, I slowly came back to Earth. My first thoughts of doing something radical had begun to run their course. I couldn't do something that would get me arrested. I was a married man and my wife depended on me to make responsible choices, to be there for her.

My next thought was of joining or starting some sort of environmental action association. We could have meeting and engage in legal protests. I went online and looked up organizations that Raven and I could be a part of, Sierra Club, 350.org, The Apollo Alliance. All of them wanted donations but not much else, and money was one thing we were short on. We had time to volunteer, but no one seemed to want that as much.

We thought of starting our own group, but what would we protest? What were we against? Carbon emissions, but whose? We were living in Carbondale Colorado at the time and I thought maybe we should protest the ski resorts in Aspen. Surely the lifts they ran were a waste of energy. But I remembered how much I love to ski and snowboard. I had a season pass to the Aspen resorts and I didn't want them to revoke it. Plus, when I thought about the issue, it seemed silly. If we were going to insist that others cut down their carbon footprints, we needed to consider our own emissions first.

Here was something we could do. Raven and I were already making use of public transportation to get to and from work. We began setting our thermostat a few degrees lower. We decided to buy organic and local food when we could. I got discouraged, though, when it came to limiting my showers. I love showering. It's a stress release for me. I can stand under the hot water for up to a half hour at a time relaxing. Buying organic food was difficult, too. We were subsisting on two teacher's salaries. We tried to buy organic produce and meat, but it was expensive, nearly twice as expensive as our ordinary grocery bills. We did what we could.

*   *   *

When I arrive at work, I receive a phone call from an old friend and roommate, Jonathan Koefoed. He'd lived with both Tim and I in a house we'd rented in Tempe while we were all students at ASU.

"I just realized the trial was going on," he says. "I've been in the U.K. for a month. What's going on?"

I fill Jonathan in on the situation. He is in touch via Facebook with another friend of ours from college who is following the trial on twitter and he passes the information I give him on. I can hear him typing furiously in the background as I talk. When I am finished telling about the trial, we talk for a while about other things. I haven't spoken to Jonathan for a long time. There's a lot to catch up on. I tell him about Ezra, and for a moment we forget about the trial, caught up in the ways life has unfolded for each of us. He asked after Raven and I asked after his wife Suzanne. Both are doing well. Suzanne is a teacher, too, in a district in Boston. Midway through telling me about her class, he groans.

"Katherine says that the verdict has just been announced. He's guilty. It's on twitter." We say goodbye quickly, promise to talk soon, hang up. I look up the twitter page to see the verdict for myself.

*   *   *

Touch

Tim was a wrestler in high school.

Wrestling is one of the most straightforward sports I can think of. Two people enter a ring and try to pin each other. There's no ball, no weapons, just hands and arms and legs and feet. Bodies pushing against each other trying to force the other wrestler to the ground. I'm sure the sport is more nuanced than that, but from what I can tell those are the basics. I was never a wrestler myself. I was a runner.

Running is simple, too. You run. Usually, you run against other runners, but you almost never come in contact with them. In fact, you try to put distance between you and your opponents. Runners do not, however, just run as fast as they can. Sprinters do that, but runners have to pace themselves, save enough of whatever is in them to last. Running is as much an internal struggle as it is a race between people. You constantly force your body to move, but also to hold back, to spend less than it could so that you don't burn out. You run against something that has no face and no name, the animal inside you that would burn you up if it could. Running is about self-control.

Wrestling is about control, too. I've watched people wrestle and in addition to incredible strength, wrestlers seem to have amazing control of their bodies. They move in ways I can't imagine, sliding sideways and under and around, applying pressure with their hips or their shoulders, and always against someone, face to face, muscle to muscle.

*   *   *

The trial is finished. Sentencing will be held the third week of June. There is still time for an appeal if Tim and his attorneys decide to launch one, of course, but even without an appeal, this is not over. The trial has resolved very little. Tim is more than just a man who broke the law. He is an activist. He has a group of supporters who have organized around him. The organization calls itself Peaceful Uprising, and they sponsor events to raise awareness about climate change and other environmental issues. Tim will continue to fight, and they will continue to fight with him.

He is a fighter by nature, a man who stands on principle. He is unaccustomed to backing down. He possesses a ruthless intelligence, amazing amounts of internal strength, and a capacity for raw emotion that I can't help but admire, and his role as an activist makes him larger than life. He is almost superhuman, a hero.

I can't help but measure myself against Tim's high standard. I am not a hero, not a fighter. I do not have Tim's ability to think on his feet. I could never speak coherently to the press. I do not believe strongly enough in any cause to endure day after day for two years. I'm not sure I could stick to my story that long. I change my mind too often.

I realize that I am something different, someone different, a different kind of activist than my friend. I am not without a kind of strength, but it seems to lie elsewhere. I am not a fighter. I find it nearly impossible to be against anything. I am against climate change of course, but it's not like you can go and knock on its door. I think about fighting against corrupt politicians, but it's corruption I'm against. I believe that people are inherently good and want to do good. I believe they are doing the best they can.

I am inclined to be for people, with people and animals and plants and Earth rather than against them. I am for my son. I am for Raven. I am for Kiribati. I am for the desert. I am for short eared owls and black bears and wolves. I cannot choose between these things, either, cannot be only for bears at the expense of people, or vice versa. I am for all of these things at once. I am in solidarity with them. It's as if we are in a race except that instead of wanting to outrun them, I simply want to keep running with them.

I think it has to do with connection. I recently heard violist Christen Lien talk about how she creates art.

"I am merely the conduit," she says. "There are things in the world and they all exist in various shapes and colors and I brush up against them and try to put what I have touched into music." I feel the same way about activism, about writing. The things I brush against are complex and I only get to touch their edges. The stories I tell are of those edges. My hope is that if I experience enough, if I write enough, maybe I can start to glimpse the whole, to see the shape of the world. This is my activism, my art. It is a long process. Perhaps there is no ending, just beginnings, over and over. A gradual movement towards one another, closer.

In the meantime, I am for Tim.

A SCENIC DRIVE DOWN ROUTE 66

Charlton Heston announced again today that he is
suffering from Alzheimer's.
> – George Clooney (National Board of
> Reviews 20th January 2003)

"There's a sale on cribs," she says, "at
Babies R Us. It's only $200 for a crib that converts
into a full size bed." I grunt in return. "That's a
really good deal."

It probably is, but I'm having trouble getting
into baby shopping. We are still six months from
having a baby, and I am alarmed by the sheer
volume of stuff that is beginning to accumulate in
preparation for our son. To be fair, we've not
bought most of it yet. A great deal of it exists only
in my mother's and mother-in-law's minds.

"Make us a list," my mother says. People
will be asking what you want soon." The idea that
other people will end up buying most of these
things for us, and an even better notion that we'll
get quite a lot of it second hand from my sister in
law who has had three babies and called it quits, is

somewhat reassuring, but the whole concept is slightly overwhelming all the same.

One needs so much shit to have a baby these days: Crib, changing table, rocking chair, high chair, swing, sling, car seat, stroller, baby carrier, diaper pail, diapers, baby bath, breast pump, bottles, bibs, nooks, outfits, pajamas, hats, bonnets, diaper bag, not to mention all the toys and books, and blankies that every member of my immediate and extended family will shortly be knitting.

"How are we supposed to know what we'll want or need," says Raven. "We've never had a baby before." I nod.

Raven has decided to go back to school a few months after having our baby. Among the schools she's looking at are University of Oregon, Arizona State, and University of New Orleans. "You're going to move right after you have a baby?" people ask, as though something like this has never been done. "I don't think you understand how much harder it is to do things like that with a baby around. You should really stay close to your parents."

Raven and I have lived without electricity or running water, hiked over two thousand miles on the Appalachian trail, and worked as educators with every age group of children there is, and yet, people insist that we are unprepared for parenthood. On one level, this scares me profoundly. On another, I question the childrearing techniques and practices of those who claim that taking care of a child is paramount to any other conceivable hardship.

There is a pervasive fear of parenthood in our culture, an anxiety that once you have children, your life will never been the same, and not in a good way. In fact, I've heard more than one person profess the view that once you have children your life is effectively over.

*   *   *

I dreamed you. You were wild haired and strange, but I knew it was you. You were naked and standing in a grove of tamarisk, almost hidden in the thick brush and in your eyes was a wildness I did not intend. I thought, oh god, what have I done, and you crouched and then leapt backwards into the river and vanished.

*   *   *

"I loved you when you were born, but I wasn't really into you. Not like I was with your sister. As soon as she came out, I was in love with her. She was so beautiful." My father smiles at this point in the retelling and it is a watery and sentimental smile. I am momentarily jealous.

"I didn't really get into you so much until you were about three years old. That winter I took you sledding. We climbed up that hill down by the bike path. The one near the soccer fields. You had this blue, plastic sled, and we got to the top and you sat down in it and I pushed you." He pauses, remembering the moment and I remember too. I can't remember the incident at all, but I remember the hill. We used to do wind sprints up it in cross country because it was the steepest hill around, and it was long, probably a hundred yards with a long, flat plain below.

"You went about 50 feet, and then the sled turned sideways and flipped and you went flying, and I thought, oh shit, he might be dead. But then you sat up in the snow and waved. I was so relieved."

"That's when you first loved your child?" My wife is incredulous. We are sitting in my parents' dining room. My mom is preparing dinner in the kitchen. The three of us are sitting around the table discussing the prospect of grandchildren.

"That was the first time I really got it, that he was a real person."

"Before that you thought he was just some kind of toy?" He shrugs and smiles in a way that says, "it is what it is." Raven looks like she wants to say something else. She's obviously upset by this information. I am surprisingly unperturbed.

*   *   *

There is a document in a locked box in my parents' basement. It's written on a comment card. "We hope you enjoyed your visit to Hogate's ----- and we'd appreciate hearing what you think of us,"

Touch

it says at the top. Underneath, in my father's somewhat untidy hand there is this:

> *After the waitress grabbed the last bite of lentil soup, the meal progressed with quite a lot of wine, shrimp, crab, and lobster. Kathy made the following on-the-record statements:*
>
> *We can go overseas (i.e., Peace Corps) after I finish nursing school.*
>
> *3 months before tour is done K. Burke goes off the contraceptives for babies.*
>
> *TJC gets the bread-winning job.*
>
> *Signed on this 9th day of June 1980*
>
> *Husband- Timothy J. Cromwell*
>
> *Wife- Kathleen A. Burke*

My dad graduated from nursing school in the spring of 1981. I was born in August of '82. They never went overseas.

*　　*　　*

"You'd better love your grandchildren instantly," says Raven, "otherwise you won't be allowed to see them."

"I'll love them," Dad says in a sappy sort of voice that is nevertheless sincere. I roll my eyes.

*   *   *

Once, my dad told me that he is filled with wanderlust. He loves to travel, especially to foreign countries. He is comfortable in the anonymity of other cultures. His social obligations and responsibilities melt away and he becomes free to remake himself. I saw his transformation when my parents visited us in Kiribati. It wasn't that he tried to fit into the local culture. He wasn't fascinated by it, nor was he frightened or nervous about making cultural blunders as Raven and I had been when we'd first arrived. Instead, he seemed to simply let go. There was a lightness to his personality I'd rarely seen before, a nonchalance. He was perfectly at ease.

My father didn't want to be a father in 1981. He wanted to travel the world. He had been a Peace Corps volunteer in Nepal in the 70s, a teacher like Raven and me, and returned to find, as we did three decades later, that America was not the place he'd thought it was. In his village, he'd lived off of seasonal vegetables, dried lentils and rice. Meat was served very occasionally for festivals and almost every bit of travelling he did had been on foot. Back at home, the sheer number of people in the stores and on the streets confused and disoriented him. Politics seemed hopelessly corrupt, and the world itself seemed unnecessarily complicated. His solution was to go back overseas. Instead, he got a job with the federal government, married my mother, and had me.

*   *   *

My grandfather breaks down slowly, a memory at a time and some of it doesn't seem like breaking down at all.

"I took a trip last summer down Route 66 he says. Me and Frank climbed into the Plymouth and drove from Chicago to California. When we got there, we split up. Frank wanted to get back to Chicago after three days, but I stayed for a month.

"There was a girl I hung around with. She was Frank's cousin and one day we were out at the beach and she had to change into her swimming outfit, so she went into a McDonalds or something and changed and when she came out, she put her bra and her panties in the glove box of the car." He pauses here and looks earnest. "So that no one would see them, you see."

He looks down and begins to pet the black lab at his side absentmindedly. "Shadow was there too. She went swimming with us and we didn't have a towel so the back seat of the Plymouth got soaked." He thinks about this for a moment.

"Actually, it wasn't the Plymouth. It was a green Ford and we'd borrowed it from Frank's aunt. Anyway, I took the cousin home and dropped her off, and the next time the aunt went to use the car, she opened the glove box and there were her daughter's underthings, and she said, 'What have you been doing in my car, Ronald?'" He laughs at this and I do too. "That was a long time ago," he says, "Back before I met your grandmother." He smiles. "I think I'll go to bed."

My grandfather pushes slowly up from the wooden chair he's in and wobbles a little. He begins walking towards his bedroom, pauses, turns aside towards the cabinets. He opens one and takes out a short glass. "You want a scotch?" he says.

"We just had one," I say. "See, your glass is over at the end of the table."

"Oh yeah," he says, and he laughs. "Well, I guess I'll have one more. You want one?"

"Alright," I say. He goes to the liquor cabinet and takes down the bottle and fills his glass, then he passes me the bottle and returns to the other end of the table. He sits down and takes a long pull of his drink.

"That's good," he says. We sit in silence for a moment, and I look around at the kitchen. It's so familiar to me. My grandparents have lived here for more than ten years and before that, every object in this kitchen had been positioned in almost the exact same arrangement as in their old house. This house is located in rural Illinois, north of Rockford. Their old house was in a suburb of Chicago. The dog, who is gray in the muzzle and rather fat, is a relatively recent acquisition. She used to live with my parents in southern Illinois. They brought her up here when they moved to Salt Lake City. Grandpa scratches her ears absentmindedly.

"Did I ever tell you about the time me and Shadow drove out to California?"

I smile.

*   *   *

Alzheimer's is a disease of affluence. My grandparents are not rich. They struggle to get by. The term is relative. It describes diseases that people are more prone to the longer they live. My grandfather has had it for almost a decade. Little by little, I see him going. He is no longer the sharp, funny man he used to be. He's lost the nuanced parts of his personality. He sleeps most of the time, waking for a few hours to eat and sit in his chair in the kitchen, and he has become dependent on my grandmother for everything.

"Grammy?" he calls plaintively, when he wants something, and she, for her part, caters to his

Touch

wishes. She cannot stand to see this man she loves so reduced. Both of them are scared and they cling to each other, to their old habits and routines, but as the disease progresses, even those get lost. The other day, my grandmother told me that he had completely forgotten who she was for the first time. She sat with him and explained that she was his wife, tried to jog his memory with photographs and the names of their children. They both ended up crying.

*   *   *

I dreamed you were the river, that the contours of its surface were rich with your laughter, that the coldness of it was the blue of your eyes. I tried to touch you, and your body swallowed my hand like water. I tried to call to you and you went on rushing away, but as I listened, the music of your movement engulfed me and I could hear the echo of your voice, singing.

*   *   *

I love my father, have always loved him, but I wasn't really "into him" for a while. Perhaps that's why I'm o.k. with the fact that he wasn't into me either. Love is a fierce emotion. It comes of instinct between parent and child, but there is a deeper kind of love more closely related to respect, which must be learned.

We used to work out together. On Sundays we would ride our bikes down to the track at SIU Edwardsville and then run a mile before biking back. I admit to being completely lame at this. My bike was slightly too big for me and I didn't understand how to work the shifters, so I rode, constantly, in one gear, simply pedaling harder on the hills.

When we got to the track, I would often whine or whimper as we ran. The mile was difficult for me. There was also this trick to mounting a bike that my dad tried to teach me. You put one foot on the pedal and push off to get going, and then swing your leg over the seat and get your other foot situated. I could not get the hang of it and refused to try.

Touch

My father got upset each time we engaged in the ritual of Biathlon Sunday. We'd start off well, but by the fourth stoplight, my awkward starts and stops would begin to get on his nerves and he would demonstrate the procedure to me over and over in the hope that I would pick it up. At the track, my whining tried his patience. On the way home, he would ridicule me about using the gears on my bike. In the end, we were both worn down.

That is how I learned to love my father. That is how he learned to love me. We wore each other down.

*   *   *

Alzheimer's is terminal, irreversible. My grandfather will die of it. It is a long time in coming, though I'll still be heartbroken when it happens. I'm heartbroken now.

I've thought that I should not have a child at all. What if I develop Alzheimer's disease and he has to care for me? What if he develops it himself? What if my worst fears come true and we are all left starving and impoverished from climate change.

And there are other more conventional terrors to be reckoned. What if he becomes a serial killer? What if he doesn't love us? "Stay in there," I think. "Just stay where you are and let us keep pretending."

I've thought these things and convinced myself that this is surely a mistake. But, he will come. Raven and I will be parents, and he will come and become. I have to hold myself back, have to breathe. It is alright not to know the future. It is alright to step into the unknown.

*   *   *

I dreamed you were an old man, far older than any I've ever met. Your hair was white and sinuous. You were from another age, and yet, you were my child, no larger than a lime, your skin translucent, your bones half formed. You were both of these at once and every age in between, and in a moment I saw your life unfold, beautiful as a monarch butterfly, strong as a redwood, deeper and more solid than a granite cliff. My fear is inconsiderate. You are enough.

*   *   *

Touch

My friend Tebwake died on Abaiang. This is how it happened. He walked out of his bathroom one morning and fell over. I saw the other men in the village running towards his house and I ran with them. He was lying on the ground, tongue lolling, eyes rolled up into his skull. I felt for a pulse. It was faint, but still present. We scooped him up into the back of a truck that had stopped near the village. I rode with him to the medical station keeping my fingers on his wrist. He was pale, chalky, his hands and feet clammy.

We massaged his extremities trying to get the blood to circulate, but the pulse got weaker and weaker and when we finally arrived at the clinic and the nurse's aide listened to his chest with her stethoscope, there was nothing to hear. Tebwake was dead. In my journal, there is a poem and a letter I wrote to my parents about the incident, how strange and spooky it was to feel a man die beat by beat and know there was nothing to be done about it.

I dwell in the aftermath of the death more than the thing itself. I stayed with the body when they brought him back to his home and watched as his wife undressed him and washed the body. She found a gray pair of briefs and slid them up over his thighs, tucked his balls into the waistband and worked the elastic over his hips and buttocks. She did this smiling, and even laughed a little while handling his genitals. It was too much for me, and I left, went back to my house, looked for something to give the dead man's family. A picture of him before he died and a frame.

I don't know the exact cause of death for Tebwake, but I'm almost certain it was massive heart failure. There was no qualified doctor on the island to perform an autopsy, and it wouldn't have mattered anyway. He died of rich food, beer, kava. He died because there was no doctor to give him a checkup. He was in his thirties.

Heart disease is also considered to be a disease of affluence though no one would argue that Tebwake was rich. It is related to poor nutritional choices. Common theories on this subject suggest that poor people don't have access to the type of diet that leads to heart attacks. Only relatively affluent societies can afford such poor nutrition.

At his wake, people took pictures of the body. Some even posed with it as though he were still alive. Raven and I could hardly keep from crying. We'd never seen something like this, so little mediation between the living and the dead.

*   *   *

Two classmates of mine died in a car accident when I was in high school. Neither of them were wearing their seat belts. I went to Marcus's wake. His body was in a casket in front of the alter of the Catholic church he attended. The attendees filed slowly past, and I had a bizarre impulse to reach out and touch his heavily made up face. He was so strange. In some ways no changes had taken place at all. He was preserved in a chemical soup, would remain sixteen forever. In other ways, he was unrecognizable. I had not known him well, but I'd seen him around, and his face was paler, puffier than it had been in life. He was stiff, had lost all the elasticity in his skin and joints, the strange spark that had made him human.

*　　　*　　　*

Tebwake began to putrefy on the second day, began turning from solid to liquid. We put him in the ground with a sense of relief.

We are not meant to be alone. We are born into relationships. Even the act of giving birth is cooperative, a negotiation between mother and child, each dependant on the other. We die in the arms of those who love us, and those left behind die a little, too.

*　　　*　　　*

I did not learn to love the desert from my father. I did not learn to love land in any form. If anything, I grew up with a kind of malice for the Earth and the things that grow upon it. I'm sure that these things seem worse in retrospect, but I remember spending most of my free time as a child on a lawn mower. We had five acres of grassy

Touch

slope as a yard and it seemed, constantly, to need mowing.

When I wasn't mowing, I was digging holes. I have a distinct memory of dad bringing home a hundred or two hundred trees, little saplings. He gave me a post hole digger and a stick with the exact width of the lawn mower deck marked on it and set me loose to dig holes for the trees with instructions to make sure they were planted far enough apart that we could still mow between them.

Other times, he would get out his chainsaw and cut down full grown trees that had died in ice storms, and buck up the logs into stove lengths. My job was to haul away all the branches that were too skinny to make into firewood to the burn pile at the far end of our property. I grew to hate poplars. Their long roots were the biggest obstacle when digging a hole, and in winter they seemed to die in scores creating piles of lumber to be hauled off.

I learned to love the desert because there was nothing to mow, no roots to dig, no timber to haul. The desert seems to resist attempts to tame it.

The thick hides of desert flora, their spines and toxins are a kind of message; they imply a code about how we should interact.

It is the intimacy between living things, the way two plants find their way around each other until cholla cannot be separated from salt brush. The way a fallen saguaro becomes a home to a rose tarantula.

I've learned to love the woods, too, as long as the trees are allowed to topple of their own accord and rot peacefully into the soil.

*   *   *

We lived close to something primal on Abaiang. Perhaps it was the fact that there was so little land and so much sea, the improbability of life itself establishing a foothold here, on such a tiny spec of land. You could not help but be awed when you stared off into the vast blue void at the tip of the island. There was a largeness to it, an immensity of scale that I cannot adequately capture.

To be that close to the edge of the world inspires a kind of connection to it. There is so little here. Literally, we were on an island of life in the middle of the sea, and we're on it still, though it is less obvious how close to the edge of the world we are. Everyone dies. My trust in the Earth stems from this. We know, irrevocably, how this is going to end, and each time it doesn't is a kind of reprieve, a stay of execution. Collectively, this defiance is what bonds us, what brings us together. It is the basis of trust, which is really only denial. These lies that we will be alright.

*   *   *

We're going with a second-hand crib. We went over and checked it out last night. Friends of ours, Larry and Jess, have a five-year-old and a three-year-old, and they're ready, at last, to give up their old things. In addition to the crib we can have our pick of diaper bags, baby carriers, a high chair, various clothes and toys.

"All this stuff is sort of overwhelming," I say. We're in Larry's kitchen. Their two kids, Marc and Eric, are in the living room watching *Dino Train*. Jess is still at work.

"It is," he says. "But you'll figure out what you need. Everyone's experience is different. When we were first pregnant with Marc, people asked us what we wanted, what we were registered for, and we were like, 'We've already got a Baby Bjorn. That's pretty much all we think we'll need.' Obviously, we were wrong, but you figure it out." We thank him and head for the door.

"Congratulations," he says, and he smiles at us with a kind of sympathy or understanding. I try my best to return the look.

"Thanks."

Once in the car, I turn to Raven. "He seemed so cheerful tonight. What's up with that?" Larry and Jess are usually aloof when we talk to them. They are of a different social caste. Jess is a doctor and Larry is an engineer, so they are rich compared with us, and they're usually too involved with their children to pay us much heed. Tonight's comments and advice are downright effusive by comparison.

"We're in the club now," says Raven. "We've been tricked into having kids too, so now there's something to talk about. Plus they're experts and they're passing on their knowledge. It always makes people keen to talk when they can dispense advice."

I am disturbed by her comments. I don't want to be "in the club." The club seems wasteful, destructive and deluded. Just think of all the crap that comes with being in the club, all the disposable diapers and clothes that get worn for a month and then thrown away. I have a brief flash of my grandfather and how all this will end.

Perhaps this shit is a substitute for a village. Perhaps it's one or the other, people or crap. I don't have a village anymore. I shake my head.

"Larry was right about one thing," I say. "We'll figure it out."

"Of course we will. Team Ben and Raven and the baby," she says, and we drive off into the night.

MWAIE

Another sleepless night. Raven's abdomen is swollen like a ripe fruit and it's getting harder and harder for her to sleep. She tosses and turns and tries to prop her abnormally large belly on the various pillows that are now a part of our bed.

Sometimes I can ignore the motion, can be soothed by it, even, and doze off into fitful dreams. Other times, she is overcome by the loneliness of being the only one awake in a dark room. I wake to the feel of a searching hand at my shoulder.

"Are you awake?" she whispers.

"yes."

We hold hands in the dark, or she lays her hand on my chest and we wait together.

We are waiting for him. It's strange to think about. He's here. He's been here the whole time, between us when we hold each other or make love, and yet he's a mystery. What will he look like? Who will he be?

We've set up his crib, washed his diapers, prepared all the things we can think of to make his transition from inside to outside as simple and easy as possible.

"We are ready for you, son," I say. But we are not. I think back to the way it was in Kiribati, to waves and sand and sky, and I can feel the steps of an ancient dance moving clumsily through my body.

We learned a mwaie, a traditional dance, while we were living in Ueen Wakaam. I have a video of the two of us, Raven and me, performing the steps in the mwaneabwa. The mwaie is based on the movements of birds and so we take small, precise steps and try to keep our bodies rigid. We move our arms like wings in strange, stiff gestures. The two of us look awkward. We are not used to the dance. We have been learning it for only two weeks. After this performance, we will not dance again. We will slowly forget the steps and the words of the song, a warrior song our teacher has informed us.

I-Kiribati men and women who are serious about the dance must be taken on by a master. Our friend, Mwaketi, is a good dancer and a fine teacher, but he admits that he is not truly qualified to pass on the semi-sacred steps of this dance. True masters are full time professionals, unimwane and unaine, old men and women who have devoted their lives to the study of movement. I've heard stories about how really dedicated dancers learn the steps. All night dance practice that takes place out in the lagoon, underwater so that the movements of the dance remain concealed until they are ready to be performed for an audience.

We are not so dedicated. We perform our dance in front of a dozen or so people to pre-recorded music. Real dancers are accompanied by a chorus of men and women singing sacred songs and pounding drums. We saw a true performance of the mwaie at a botaki in a village north of ours. The dancers were beautiful, their long dark hair rippling about their shoulders, the sheen of it, bright in the light of a dozen lanterns. Their movements spoke of power, of the wind and sea, of an austere economy in which nothing is wasted.

The performance occurred in cycles, three rounds of progressively faster and louder singing, faster and faster dancing. At one point, one of the dancers began to wail. I thought she must be upset at making some sort of mistake, but her dancing seemed as flawless as that of any of the other dancers.

The movements became faster, more frantic as the song neared an end and her wailing devolved into shrieks of agony or ecstasy, I couldn't tell which, and then she collapsed and lay writhing on the floor, wailing and moaning at the top of her lungs. It was alarming and almost comical, but also beautiful in a way.

Before we saw this performance, we'd heard about the spirit of the dance, about how men and women can sometimes become so caught up in the momentum of movement, that they are overcome by it. The reality of this spiritual tempest was more intense than I had ever imagined it could be. I had dismissed it as some sort of religious mumbo jumbo, a performance, like speaking in tongues, which one does because there are people watching and it legitimizes the faith of fellow believers.

I suppose the spirit of the dance could have been something like that, performed for our benefit, but I don't think so.

Instead, I think that the mwaie is rooted in the island, in the sand and sea, in the bush. It is an expression of the deepest nature of Kiribati, based on the birds and trees and cycles of the ocean, and its most devoted adherents, make themselves conduits for the island. They give it sentience, a human outlet.

I think the spirit of the dance is the expression of a vast, powerful force working its way out through a person's body. It is fierce, uncontrollable, and awful in its true form.

One can learn the steps, but one can never be truly prepared.

*   *   *

Touch

We made love in the middle of the night, in the sweltering heat of late July. We were wrapped in each other's bodies, legs curled around buttocks, arms enfolding shoulders and hair, skin moving on skin, and as we moved, we laughed, and as we sweated, we sang, and as we held each other in the moment of climax, we were overcome with shrieks and wailing and collapsed into each other as though a new kind of gravity had suddenly sprung up between us, as though we could never be separated from one another again.

*　　*　　*

Ezra breaks over us like waves from the epicenter of an earthquake. We are utterly overcome. I call out to him, but my son does not respond to my voice, except to shift positions inside Raven's belly. I see the tiny dome of a foot or a knee through the skin. I place my hand on him and he settles, trembling with the power of his own beating heart.

Soon.

THE LAKE CARLISLE MONSTER

If you listen, I'll save your life. If you don't listen,
I'll die. Also, if you don't listen, you'll die a lot
harder. There's the exchange.
    –David Shields (from *Reality Hunger*)

I will tell just one more story.

This is a version of the tale my father used
to tell me when I was a child. It has a strange and
particular meaning for me, now, as I become a
father myself. I've begun to dream the story a few
times a week, and I wake up shaking with the voice
of the monster in my head. The eyes, burning in my
mind like the afterimage of a bright light. Perhaps
it is simple anxiety prompting the dreams, but I
have a feeling it may run deeper, to the heart of my
fear.

I give this story to you as a warning, and as
a talisman, and as a way to be rid of it myself. I
want to haunt you.

*   *   *

Once upon a time, a man and his son
decided to go camping. They packed their things, a

tent, some sleeping bags and pillows, flashlights and food, into the back of an old yellow pickup truck and drove up to a campground on the banks of Lake Carlisle.

After they set up the tent, the boy felt hungry and so they built a fire and took out an old metal pot to make stew. It was twilight as the man and boy set off down a path near their site to find water for the stew. The boy carried the pot and the man carried a flashlight. As they walked it grew darker and darker until it was almost too dark to see, but before the man could turn on his flashlight, there appeared before them a pair of glowing yellow eyes.

The man took a half step forward and placed his free hand on the boy's shoulder and drew him near. They both stood that way, frozen in the glare of those eyes, and in the silence, the owner of the eyes let out a low growl.

"I know who you are." The voice of the beast was low and gravelly and it sent chills down their arms. The man shuddered in the darkness, but he tried to stay calm for the boy's sake. He knew there were bears in the area and he decided to make a disturbance to try and make this one leave. He clicked on the flashlight and shone it where the creature's body should have been.

All they saw in the light of the beam, was deeper shadow.

"I know who you are," the creature said, in a louder voice, and again, the man suppressed an involuntary spasm of fear. Bears, he thought, could not speak.

He thought, briefly, of making a run for it. Perhaps he could scoop the boy into his arms and sprint back to the tent before the creature caught them. He thought, too, of the warm fire awaiting them back at the campsite, and of his truck and his home and his wife who would miss them, husband and son, if they were eaten out here in the woods.

Alright, alright, he thought. If it comes to that, then it comes to that.

"I know who you are," said the monster again, not from the lake but from the woods, and it was like a roar now, and the man moved his son more fully behind him in the darkness.

"What are you?" The man said it out loud to the night.

His voice sounded strong and clear to his own ears and that gave him some comfort. He sounded braver than he felt, though. He waited for a moment, half expecting an answer, and half expecting to be set upon by whatever was out there with the glowing yellow eyes.

It could have been an owl or a raccoon or a wolf or a bear, but it wasn't. Disturbing as wild animals could be, they did not absorb light, and they could not speak, only growl and the words were too distinct not to trust his ears.

The man thought of the words. This black hearted creature claimed to know him. Was it an evil spirit or a devil. Was it a demon of some kind, or a sasquatch that knew only those five words.

"You don't know me," the man said, and again his voice was confident. How could the monster know him? He surely didn't know the monster. He was fairly sure he didn't believe in monsters. "I don't believe in monsters," he said, and he laughed heartily, and if it sounded a bit forced, who could blame him?

He looked at the creature, feeling reckless and wild, as one does just before a fight. The eyes sat motionless for several seconds, and the man thought he might have to make the first move. He might lunge into the darkness at whatever this was and try to punch it. He steeled himself for the act, but just as he tensed his muscles, the eyes winked out, disappeared into the blackness.

The man and the boy looked around, shining the flashlight into the trees, but the monster was gone. All they could see was woods and all they could hear was the faint trickling of water from the stream up ahead.

"What should we do now?" asked the boy.

The man thought for a moment. He thought perhaps the thing was still out there in the darkness lurking out of sight, but as he shined the light into the stand of trees and saw nothing, he began to doubt himself. Perhaps the monster had been some sort of trick. He took the boy's hand.

"C'mon," said the man, and they walked on towards the sound of trickling water.

That night, after they'd eaten their stew and roasted marshmallows and sung some songs, the boy and the man had a good laugh about the monster. The man had managed to convince the boy that it was all just a practical joke, and it was easy to believe that it was in the light of a brightly burning campfire. They climbed into their sleeping bags and snuggled close to the fire, and the boy fell asleep. The man watched his breathing deepen as the firelight flickered lower and lower.

Unbidden, the image of those glowing yellow eyes came back into his mind. He wasn't scared of them. He hadn't even been that scared of them at the time. They'd been an illusion. But they'd seemed real... too real.

And the voice had been close and breathy, as intimate as a caress.

He shivered. The darkness and the dying firelight were conspiring to make him doubt the story he'd told to comfort his son. It seemed thin and feeble as an explanation, now. Who would go to that sort of trouble to scare a couple of campers?

His eyes fell on the boy again, and he gave a shudder. What if the eyes had been real, he thought, and then, on the heels of that thought: What if the eyes and the voice hadn't been meant for him? What if they were meant for the boy? Perhaps those words had a special meaning not for him, but for his son.

Immediately he clicked on his flashlight and searched the surrounding darkness. There was nothing. He found another log and added it to the fire. It caught and the light burned brighter, but all this served to do was make the shadows more menacing. The man drew his sleeping bag up behind his son and lay down by him. He put his arm over the boy and propped his head up on his other elbow, watching.

Touch

They stayed that way all night, the boy breathing deep and steady and the man guarding him. There was no sign of the yellow eyes that night, and in the morning they packed and drove home.

*   *   *

I used to imagine myself as the child in the story, but in my dreams, I've become the father.

My son, Ezra, has passed the danger point. He's seven and a half months along. If he were born today, he'd have a very good chance of survival. My fears for him have evolved from those of premature birth to something deeper and more sinister. There will always be things out there in the dark, and in the dream, just like real life, it's my job to protect him.

The obvious interpretation of these dreams is that the monster with the glowing eyes is climate change. It is indistinct, hard to wrap my mind around, and it is personal. It knows me, knows just where I am most vulnerable, and that is where it will strike. It is threatening, but when I approach it, it seems to slip away leaving only its tracks.

I am fascinated by horror stories, the psychological elements of trying to confront the unknown. I am divided in my loyalties between the protagonists and the monsters. I want them to be real and at the same time, I know that if they were, I might never sleep again.

The story of the Lake Carlisle Monster has no resolution. It ends there, in the woods, with a beast hiding somewhere in the shadows. This is where we are. Even if we are able to change the tide of rising global temperatures, the monsters will always be out there. Greed, corruption, apathy. These things reside in the deepest parts of human nature and can only be confronted, never defeated.

The stories I know by heart, the ones I've told myself over and over again, are about courage, about stepping forward into the unknown. The monsters never really go away. They are out there in some form or another. The trick is to push down the mounting panic and look them in the eyes.

Touch

EPILOGUE

His eyes are beautiful, liquid, changing things. One moment they are a dark bluish gray. The next I think I see copper at their centers. They boil like storm clouds, resolving in a moment so that I think I know how they will turn out, and then turning, again, into unresolved depths.

He is so beautiful, so perfect. His body sits in the crook of my arm, long and lean and relaxed, a peaceful expression on his face. We stare at each other for hours learning anew what the world is. That it is not all disaster and fear. No, not so bad as all that.

It is dark hair, matted and thin. It is limbs stretched out into the air with inexpert grace. It is trust, instinctive and unearned. The ways we touch each other.

*   *   *

Begin again.

SELECTED BIBLIOGRAPHY

Abbey, Edward. *Desert Solitaire: A Season in the Wilderness*. New York, NY: McGraw-Hill, 1986. Print.

Dillard, Annie. *Pilgrim at Tinker Creek*. New York, NY: Harper Collins, 1974. Print.

"I Get a Kick Out of You." *Economist*. www.economist.com, 12 February 2004. Web. 2 November 2010.

Lilly, Ray. "Study: Coral Atolls Hold On Despite Sea Level Rise." *The Huffington Post*. www.huffingtonpost.com, 3 June 2010. Web. 5 September 2010.

Louv, Richard. *Last Child in the Woods: Saving Our Children from Nature-Deficit Disorder*. Chapel Hill, NC: Algonquin Books, 2005. Print.

McManus, Justin. "Pacific Island Sinking." *The Guardian*. www.Gurdian.co.uk, 8 November 2010. Web. 10 November 2010.

Muir, John. *A Thousand-Mile Walk to the Gulf*. Boston, MA: Houghton Mifflin Company, 1916. Print.

Nordhaus, Ted. *Break Through*. Boston, MA: Houghton Mifflin Company, 2007. Print.

Orr, David. *Down to the Wire*. Cary, NC: Oxford University Press, 2009. Print.

Solnit, Rebecca. *A Field Guide to Getting Lost*. New York, NY: Viking, 2005. Print.

Solnit, Rebecca. *Hope in the Dark*. New York, NY: Nation Books, 2004. Print.

Sustein, Cass. *Risk and Reason*. Cambridge, U.K.: Cambridge University Press, 2002. Print.

Thoreau, Henry David. *Walden and Civil Disobedience*. New York, NY: Barnes and Noble Books, 2003. Print.

Thoreau, Henry David. *Walking*. 1862. Transcendentalists.com. Accessed 9/25/10. Web.

Thoreau, Henry. *The Maine Woods*. New York, NY: Harper and Row, 1987. Print.

Williams, Terry Tempest. *Refuge*. New York, NY: Pantheon Books, 1991. Print.

Wilson, E.O. *Biophilia*. Boston, MA: Harvard University Press, 1984. Print.